THE
SEAGULL

*Stories of those
who dared to fly higher*

MARGARET PEAT

Acknowledgements

I would especially like to thank David and Jan Holdaway for their advice, patience and expertise in helping to publish this book.

First Published October 2008, by Life Publications, Merthyr Tydfil, South Wales, UK.

Cover design by Graham Alder
Contact: KMPeat@aol.com

Life Publications

Comments about Margaret's first book –
The White Elephant

"Thank you so much for your amazing book Margaret...I have read it and found it really encouraging. It is very moving. Thank you for writing it."
MS

"I couldn't put your book down, in fact I'm going to get another copy for my sister, where can I get one from?" SS

"Many, many thanks for your book. It is a bobby-dazzler. We both enjoyed the talks, so down to earth, so real. I am not just saying this, I really mean it. I am sure the Good Lord will bless and use this effort for His work."
DH

"I thought I would e-mail you to say your book is amazing. I never read books because I don't find them easy but I have read your whole book and it is great. I am now going to read it again and work through the exercises. I am so excited about going through it again to see the growth in the future. Your book puts things across so simply but deep. Thank you so much."
PW

"I bought one of Margaret's books for a lady I have been visiting in the community. The woman has accepted Jesus and I am continuing to meet with her on a weekly basis. This woman has had a very difficult time for many years and has been struggling terribly. The book was very helpful and allowed me to share with her. She really enjoyed it and I have since bought another one for someone else. I just thought you would be encouraged."
TP

"Your book is brilliant and really well done!"
CA

"Well, what can I say? Through the tears and the laughter, my only criticism is that it was not long enough. I couldn't wait to get to the next story. Looking forward to book two."
AW

"I've started reading the book. I'm really impressed. I find it simple in its readability, yet profound in its content."
SF

"Thank you so much for writing your book – best book I've read in ages, honestly. You mentioned at the beginning what one needed when reading the book. You omitted box of tissues! I bawled – especially in the first chapter. God challenged me right there and then and further healing was done in me. I may well use the book as a basis for small group studies with women or on a one to one, at some future date."
VR

"What a wonderful book! Thank you."
RG

"I read your book for my holiday reading and I found it very good. It was very encouraging and helpful. A few chapters brought a tear to my eye, even the first chapter. Thank you, Margaret. When is book two on the shelf?"
MR

"Before another day goes by, I must write to tell you how awesome your book is. It is fantastic! What a great book, I could hardly put it down. I love true stories and the stories were not only very interesting, but powerful in their lessons

and very well written. I had no idea you were such a good writer! Another thing, I felt your heart in each page. It was your heart, so close and keenly connected to the Father's heart, that came through the pages. I wept a few times. I would like to take 20 copies back to Canada."
PB

"I have just read your book which my wife gave as part of my Christmas presents. This is a really Holy Spirit inspired way in which to share the truths you do. The book has been a special blessing to me."
GH

"Started to read your book and even the first chapter made me cry. Think I'm going to love this book."
SW

"I have heard so many positive feedbacks regarding your book. I think it would be great for you to do another."
DH

Commendations

"This is a startling and inspiring collection of faith raising testimonies – beautifully told and full of moving and memorable moments. I didn't think it was possible to improve on Margaret's first volume, "The White Elephant." But this is even better! I highly recommend it."

Dr Mark Stibbe is the Vicar of St Andrew's Church, Chorleywood, a large and growing charismatic Anglican Church just outside London. He is the best-selling author of numerous works, and he regularly speaks about the father heart of God and the healing of the orphan heart.

"Margaret writes from the heart and speaks to the spirit. Her poignant stories describe in un-religious language those powerful intersections between God and people. These stories will captivate you, convict you, and challenge you to come up higher. I love your new book Margaret, don't stop writing!"

Betsy Kylstra is the joint founder and overseer of Proclaiming His Word Ministries which is dedicated to bringing healing and freedom to the Body of Christ.

"You will find yourself taking an inward journey as you read this book. You'll be challenged by areas in your life, past and present, that need a touch from God. Margaret's writing style allows for you to be drawn into the people sharing their stories. While you read their stories, listen to what God is saying to you!"

Steve Long, with his wife Sandra, is the Senior Pastor of Toronto Airport Christian Fellowship, Toronto, Canada. He works particularly in the areas of inner healing, deliverance, and physical healing.

*I would like to dedicate this book
to all herein, who have flown to higher
realms and now wait in His presence...
till we fly together again...*

Contents

Foreword

It has been a delight to receive the many positive comments and observations following the publication of my first book, *The White Elephant*.

It has been exciting to hear of copies passed to un-churched friends, to those in crisis, used in housegroups, purchased for churches, passed to Glaswegian and Scottish colleagues and used in many other ways.

This second book, *The Seagull*, deals with eleven more issues of the heart.

Each chapter shares a person's story from our time in Glasgow, followed by some practical ways to help you focus more personally and allow God to dig in the garden of your heart.

Take time to allow God to impact you in whatever way He chooses. Give Him permission to go to work in your heart in a deeper way than ever before.

These are exciting days and it is my heartfelt prayer that you will fly higher through reading this book.

Margaret

The Seagull

The Beach

I continued to walk along the beach.

My eyes were fixed on a small object some eight hundred yards ahead of me. It was perched on a cliff at the end of the expanse of sand. I continued to move closer, my eyes never leaving the object in view. Even though it was summer in the Shetland Isles, the wind was chilly on my skin as I stood on the beach.

Some ten minutes later, I stood below the large bird's nest which was secured in a crack in the cliff which towered above me. Suddenly, from nowhere, a huge seagull flew close, circled a couple of times and then landed on the edge of the nest above me. It busied itself for a moment and then as I watched, it soared once again into the sky. The seagull flew into the distance and then I turned once again and looked up.

I could hear a faint noise and as I looked more closely, I could see a small, furry creature, awaiting the return of its mother with more food.

I returned to visit the tiny seagull every day of my holiday. Each day it grew a little more and I really hoped to see it climb to the edge of the nest and maybe even to fly.

The Seagull

On the last day, I waited longer than usual, just in case the little bird chose that day to take its biggest step in life. Nevertheless, a few minutes later, I found myself walking back along the sand, disappointed that I would never see my seagull fly.

Way down the beach, I turned to look at the nest for the last time.

"You're going to see that seagull fly...and you're going to fly too..."

Suddenly I heard the voice of God speak in my spirit. I heard it, and as I returned home, I kept it in my heart.

...

It was in October that we unexpectedly returned to the island. My first act was to walk along that same beach. I reached the end of the sand and stood once again under the nest. I waited a few minutes, looking up at the nest. It seemed to me that no one lived there any more. But, suddenly, a young, strong bird flew down out of the sky and landed on the edge of the nest. As I watched, I knew it was my seagull.

"You're going to see your seagull fly...and you're going to fly too..."

Those words came back to me in a flash. I knew they were true and however it would take place, I wanted it to happen.

I looked around where I stood, at the white sand and the blue sky, white clouds and fresh air. It was God's land and it was a lovely place to be. But I knew it was also God's land where I lived too. Among the tall tenements of Glasgow, the hustle and bustle of city life and the thousands of people, there too, were people who were learning to fly.

I wanted to watch the young seagull fly again and again, but eventually I turned and walked back up the beach.

The Beach

Arriving at the cottage, I opened the door and went inside.

...

In your hand are stories of people who have learned to fly. You will see them negotiate problems and challenges and struggle with all manner of things but you will also see many of them fly.

Take time to allow their stories to inspire you and allow God to minister to you on your own journey to soar.

The Seagull

Chapter 1

Billy and Ben
Jim's Story

The effect of attitude

I looked at the two white, furry creatures in front of me, and they in turn, regarded me cautiously. It was the first time that I had been face to face with rats! I did not move and neither did they, until a noise came from the door and then glancing over, they ran to the figure in the doorway.

Several times Kevin had invited me to meet Billy and Ben but each time, up until this point, I had politely declined. Billy and Ben lived with Jim Shields. Jim had been widowed for several years, and the three of them lived happily together in the west of the city of Glasgow.

Strangely enough, a few days before I was due to meet Billy and Ben, I came across an article about rats. It was not a subject which would normally form part of my reading matter but on this occasion, I continued to read on.

"Did you know that rats can laugh?" I shouted into the kitchen to Kevin.

"Sorry?" he replied.

"Rats," I repeated, "they can laugh. Apparently they give out 'socially induced vocalization' when they are playing together and if you tickle them, it happens then too."

"Well Jim's rats certainly enjoy a tickle," Kevin said, entering the room with a glass of juice.

"Yes," I continued. "Humans can't hear the noise, but they say it's a response to being tickled or to when they are expecting something rewarding."

"So that means they've got a sense of humour?" Kevin asked sitting on the chair opposite the television.

I read some more.

"No, it says that the research was unable to prove they have a sense of humour but it did indicate rats can laugh and express joy," I finished.

By that time the television was on and Kevin was somewhere in the Middle East.

Once in Jim's apartment, Billy and Ben looked just like your common old street rats, but they were much more than that. As tame as little dogs, within a little while, they were sitting on my knee being hand fed nuts and other goodies.

Before we had arrived, I wasn't sure that I even wanted to be in the same room as them but here I was within minutes, stroking them, feeding them and laughing at their crazy antics. I watched as the small creatures ran around the neat little room in search of entertainment. I had to admit having them sit on my knee and feeding them a nut was one thing, but watching Kevin and Jim have them crawling up their arms and round their neck was another!

Jim sat in his favourite chair by the window. His high rise flat looked down onto the Ibrox Football Stadium.

There are five senior soccer clubs in Glasgow – Rangers, Celtic, Clyde, Partick Thistle and Queen's Park. The last, the oldest and only amateur team in Britain to play in a professional league.

In 1872, Queen's Park supplied all 11 players for the Scottish International team. Since then it is Rangers and Celtic which have risen to major heights within the game.

Ibrox Stadium is the home of Glasgow Rangers founded in 1873. Celtic Park in Parkhead, is the home of Glasgow Celtic founded 15 years later in 1888.

Amazingly enough, the church was equal distance from both and exactly in the middle of the two. We liked to think, when we watched our people, both Catholics and Protestants join together as family as they met God as a reality, that it was a bridge between the two religious extremes of the city. Which was represented by these two football clubs.

I took a sip of my Irn Bru as I continued to look across the room at this ordinary man who was a most extraordinary individual.

As we got to know him better, we found Jim had reached the age of 63 when his wife was severely disabled by a stroke. Jim had cared for her daily over a number of years until sadly, she passed away.

Alone in the world, he might have been bitter, but if anything it was the opposite. A man who sowed into the lives of everyone he met, he became a magnet for people. You would find Jim, Sunday by Sunday, standing at the door of the church waiting to welcome people into the service. Slender build, grey hair, grey well trimmed beard, he became a familiar face to all in the Glasgow Church. Well spoken and with impeccable manners, he carried out his tasks week by week.

Jim was also a photographer and there was one occasion we had planned to have a presentation of photographs set to music, showing some of the more sad sights of Glasgow. We thought this was a great idea and sent Jim off with a long list of required photos necessary for our film. Jim arrived in the city centre and spent the day following round pigeons, homeless people, policemen, vagrants, shoppers and all we had written on his list.

All went well until late afternoon when he was nearly arrested taking a photograph of a sex shop and almost spent the night in the police cells. Only his excellent communication skills convinced the policeman that he was out on behalf of a church and not camping outside the shop for other more dishonourable reasons! I smiled as I remembered that time.

I watched as Billy jumped from the floor to the chair and then crawled across the table and sat on a large knife. The knife was a Gurkha knife and Jim had just fetched it from the bedroom. We each looked closely at it before he laid it on the table. We sat while he told us its amazing story.

"We had landed behind enemy lines a few weeks earlier," he began, with a faraway look in his eyes. "I was in the Chindits (Allied Special Force during World War 2) and we had been in Burma a while. It was our mission to attack the enemy on his territory and attempt to disrupt his supply chains. Obviously, it was the mission of the Japanese soldiers to hunt us down and so for British soldiers to get out again was very difficult and often rare."

I listened intently as I watched Billy settle down comfortably on the blade and close his eyes. Jim continued.

"There was one particular morning when I was on radio duty and all seemed unnervingly quiet. Suddenly, I heard a noise behind me. I didn't have time to see the Japanese soldier, bayonet in hand, moving towards me. All I felt was a sharp stab in my back as the bayonet pierced my flesh and then everything went black. Another thing I didn't see was a Gurkha soldier enter almost simultaneously through the door, and swing his Gurkha knife through the air – I didn't see what happened to the Japanese soldier. I'm glad I didn't," he laughed.

"It was a few days later," he continued, "That I was lying on the makeshift bed on the floor of the jungle when in walked the very Gurkha who saved my life! He came over to where I lay and stood above me, knife in hand. It was the custom of the Gurkhas to present the knife to the life they have saved and so hence here it is – the very knife."

We looked at the Gurkha knife sitting on the table with Billy asleep on it and were silent for a few minutes.

Jim had many stories, all true, all intensely interesting. He listened to the pilots and to air traffic control as the aeroplanes flew overhead – he became an extra in films and he was a wealth of information about many subjects.

A little while later, Kevin and I were sitting in the middle of George Square, on a sunny day. The twelve statues in the square of Walter Scott, Queen Victoria, Robert Burns and others stared silently down on us. The city chambers, complete with its three statues of Truth, Riches and Honour, stood at the head of the square while Queen Street Train Station stood at the corner of the other end.

Suddenly, the mobile phone began to ring and Kevin retrieved it from his pocket and put it to his ear. It was about Jim. He had been burgled and many of his possessions had gone. We knew this was not the first time, in fact over the last few months, he had been burgled a total of three times.

"The knife's away," Jim said, as we spoke with him a day later. And it wasn't just the knife, but his medal and precious things of his wife and many other treasures too. And yet Jim, in his usual calm way, simply looked across the room at us and smiled. Never one to fuss or flap, always thinking the best even in the most difficult of circumstances, quiet, unassuming and yet always sowing good into the lives of those he met.

Ten years on, Jim moved into an area where he doesn't worry about burglaries and bumps in the night. Now, a sprightly 82 year old, surrounded by close friends of all ages, he is reaping what he has sown over many years. I will never forget his words of testimony one cold November night at the church:

"I've got so many things in my life to thank God for. Not just the good things. I thank God for the bad things as well because there's a purpose in all of them. For many of them, I've seen the purpose, for others they'll be revealed to me when I'm in glory myself. I've no family as such. I lost my step-daughter a few months ago. I was an only child. I have no children of my own but in all of you here I have the greatest family God could ever give me. I have friends whom I love. I thank God for that, and I thank God for you listening."

But that was Jim. Nothing on earth could quell his thankfulness in good circumstances and bad. As for Billy and Ben, they have moved on to an even better home in the sky with an abundance of nuts and everything they could need. At least that's what I like to think.

...

Are there times when you'd really like to change your circumstances? Do you have situations in your life which you'd rather not walk through? God doesn't always change your circumstances, but He can change your heart.

We have no power over people or events but we do have power over how we feel, because every positive and negative feeling is a direct result of our thoughts. Our feelings respond to our thoughts. It is our thinking, not our circumstances that determine how we feel.

Why don't you, at this moment, bring your thoughts afresh under His Lordship and from now on, make a choice to ask God to minister to your attitude and change it today?

Prayer:

Father, your word clearly tells me that just as Jesus suffered pain, that at times, I must be ready to suffer too. And right at this moment, I want to lay before you those things in my life which cause me pain. (List those things now)

Lord, you know it is my desire that you rescue me from this fire. I know, Lord, you are able, but if not, then right now, knowing you are by my side, I make a choice to be content within my situation, knowing you will bring me through. Father, open my eyes to show me your blessings right now, in Jesus' name. Amen.

Now take time to allow Him to place in your mind, blessings in your life, your favourite person, a holiday, a child or whatever. Whatever He shows you, thank Him and do this daily over the next month. Take some time now, with Him.

	The Truth about your Attitude
Proverbs 14:30	A sound mind makes for a robust body, but runaway emotions corrode the bones.
Romans 14:17-18	God's kingdom isn't a matter of what you put in your stomach, for goodness sake. It's what God does with your life as He sets it right, puts it together, and completes it with joy. Your task is to single-mindedly serve Christ. Do that and you'll kill two birds with one stone: pleasing the God above you and proving your worth to the people around you.
Romans 15:4b	God wants the combination of His steady, constant calling and warm, personal counsel in scripture to come to characterize us, keeping us alert for whatever He will do next.
Philippians 4:6-7	Don't fret or worry; instead of worrying, pray. Let petitions and praises shape your worries into prayers, letting God know your concerns. Before you know it, a sense of God's wholeness, everything coming together for good, will come and settle you down. It's wonderful what happens when Christ displaces worry at the centre of your life.
Philippians 4:8	Summing it all up, friends, I'd say you'll do best by filling your minds and meditating on things true, noble, reputable, authentic, compelling, gracious, the best, not the worst; the beautiful, not the ugly; things to praise, not things to curse.
1Peter 4:1-2	Since Jesus went through everything you're going through and more, learn to think like Him. Think of your sufferings as a weaning from that old sinful habit of always expecting to get your own way. Then you'll be able to live out your days free to pursue what God wants instead of being tyrannized by what you want.

Personal Notes:

The Seagull

Chapter 2

A Mansion in Heaven
Dolly's Story

Ungodly beliefs

A t last, I could see I had her attention.

"But what about Sally?" I repeated. "You are the only person she has in the whole world," I continued.

Dolly regarded me silently as I went on. "Think of her start in life, she has at last found happiness with you. At last, she has a real home of her own. Could you take that away from her?"

I knew I was winning for that day. Sally was Dolly's little dog. She had owned her for a few months now and I was using this little stray as a reason for Dolly to live.

We sat on the steps at the front of the church in the rare afternoon sunshine. We had been deep in conversation for a while when I had the brainwave about the dog. Life was tough for Dolly. She had come a long way, a long, long way and yet still there were times she was desperate and felt like ending it all.

This was one of these times and as we were chatting I was searching for a reason for her to continue. Dolly regarded me steadily.

"There is that, hen," she replied at last and that was all she said but I knew in her eyes the urge had died once again, at least for this time.

We talked for a while longer. She explained how she never felt good enough to receive anything from God. She felt that years of her life had been wasted and it was too late to change it. We sat in the sun while she talked of the many ungodly beliefs which ruled her life and how she needed her belief system renewing by the truth of the Word of God.

It was strange how close she felt to this little scrap of animal life. Both starting out in abuse and misery, both finding each other and in it, finding a better life. They provided for each other something that cared, a reason to live.

Dolly had begun life as an orphan and had joined the orphanage when she was just weeks old. There have been many Catholic children's homes, some good and some bad. This one was bad. Through those years in the home, it seemed that Dolly was on a downward spiral. She felt isolated and rejected and that she belonged to no one. She believed she was worthless and inferior. Abuse and ill treatment were common place and it seemed there was no way out.

We first met Dolly on a Monday morning when she wandered into the church building. It was Kevin's day off but we had called at the church to drop off some papers and we were just closing the office door when she wandered up the corridor.

"Please help me. Please help me," she slurred. It was obvious even at this time in the morning she was truly worse the wear for drink.

"Please help me," she continued as she slowly made her way down the corridor towards where we stood. Kevin gently moved forward and took her arm, leading her back towards the office door. Once seated inside, we began to talk.

That was our first encounter with this special lady. Always dressed in baggy trousers, and a baseball cap, Dolly no longer had any hair. Alopecia had robbed her of that. From a distance and even sometimes close up, she could hardly be identified as a woman at all. Every feminine attribute seemed removed or at least well hidden from view. Her eyes were bright blue but in them could be seen a mirror of the life she had known thus far.

It was a couple of years later when I walked into the church one Thursday night after the weekly prayer meeting. It had obviously been a lively night as various people were still sitting, standing and lying in various places in the room still very much in the presence of God. I glanced around the room and saw Kevin was at the front of the church still praying for a few people. As I began to walk down the aisle towards him I glanced to my left. There on the chair, laid across four chairs was Dolly. I couldn't tell whether she was overcome with the Spirit of God or the spirit of the world at that moment, but I did see someone standing above here. It was Alan.

Alan was a leader in our church. Always full of faith, he was fervently praying for Dolly's release from the chains in which she found herself. I watched for a moment and then continued down the aisle.

"I see Dolly's getting prayer," I said to Kevin as I reached him at the front.

"Yes, she's been there all evening, and so has Alan," he replied as he collected his Bible and notes from the lectern.

"All evening?" I repeated.

"All evening," he replied. We walked towards the door at the back of the sanctuary and as I glanced behind me, I saw Alan still praying.

It was a week later that I heard Dolly hadn't touched drink since the prayer. At first the doubt in me rose and I thought surely that can't be true? But sure enough, something that night had been broken, and she began the upward climb towards her dream.

The changes came one by one. Aided by Alan and also by Angela, another treasure amongst our people, Dolly was soon installed in her own little tenement flat in a street near to the church. She had her own cooker, fridge, bed and television for the first time in many years.

The second thing to arrive was a job. It was an unpaid job, but Dolly didn't worry and as she helped in the Glasgow City Mission she showed care and compassion to all she met. Slowly, just very slowly, we saw the truth of the Father begin to permeate her mind and to speak to her of the truth about herself. That she was bought with a price and that she mattered to God.

Next came the family. Little Sally arrived one wet winter's night. Transformed in an evening from a number in a cage to number one dog, proud owner of new bowl, basket, blanket and ball, black and white Sally came to love her new life. And it seemed Sally loved Dolly as much as Dolly loved Sally. And so one became two.

Two months on, I was present as Dolly stepped up to the microphone one dark Sunday night in November. This was her moment to share what her God had done in her life. I smiled as the Glasgow people began to cheer when Kevin announced her name. As she stepped forward, the baggy trousers were replaced by a dress and the baseball cap was gone and in its place a beautiful wig of brown styled hair. I couldn't believe my eyes. I caught the faces of Angela and Alan through the crowd as they watched her begin, and I knew that they felt as I felt, and no doubt a lot more besides.

It was three months later when I stood waiting for Glasgow's Clockwork Orange, the subway opened in 1896, the world's oldest underground system. I stood waiting for the bright orange train, looking in both directions at the two lines which go round in a circle in opposite directions. Suddenly, my mobile phone rang. I heard a worried voice as I answered the phone. I continued to listen.

"She'd never ever have left Sally," I could hear the tremor in Angela's voice as she spoke. Angela was in the process of explaining quickly how she had not heard from Dolly for a couple of days, quite unusual for her, and on investigation at the flat, she found one hungry little dog and no Dolly. I knew in my heart that something must be wrong. Dolly lived for that dog. She would defend it with her life. To leave the animal alone for days with no food would be unthinkable in her mind.

I pressed the off button on my phone, now quite worried myself, and waited. It was later that evening that Angela rang to give us the news that Dolly had been found dead in her home. Obscured by the bed, she was not seen from the main part of the room. It was a policeman who found her that evening. Tears rolled down my cheeks as I remembered how she walked round that home with pride, how she learned to care for her small animal, how she walked with her God through those months.

My mind went back to the night Dolly stood on the platform one winter's night and shared her story:

"I moved here on Christmas day and I knew what the Christian life was all about. I knew about it but doing something about it was something different for me. In actual fact I was playing a game. Just a few months ago, I gave my life to the Lord, properly this time and I meant it. I truly have seen some tremendous changes in my life. The first five months in the hostel, I didn't eat or anything, I just drank myself stupid. I had no self respect, no self esteem, no nothing. But I know God is working in my life. I'm not very good at words but I know He is and I can feel the difference. Next week, I'll be six months sober thank God and it's only with His help."

I remembered how the people clapped and clapped because they too had seen the transforming power of God at work in this body and mind.

I knew that there was no better place for her to go from, into the arms of the Father, than the place that she loved, with a church family who loved her and a little dog who gave her that unconditional love that little dogs give.

(For all dog lovers, Sally found another very special home too.)

No doubt Dolly enjoyed moving into her mansion in heaven even more than her home on earth. I pray she did and when I see her again she can show me round!

...

Do you find that the shadows of the past have left imprints on your mind? Do you find that your beliefs about yourself and about others' actions towards you, so often do not match up to what God's Word has to tell you? That your ungodly beliefs affect who you are, how you see yourself, how you relate to others and how you relate to God? Our belief affects our expectations in life. Our expectations affect our behaviour and our behaviour affects our experience. Our experience then goes on to confirm our beliefs and the cycle then repeats itself.

That is how your ungodly beliefs reaffirm themselves again and again through experience. Even as mature Christians, we can have thoughts flashing through our mind when difficult circumstances occur and a new layer of ungodly beliefs are revealed.

Is it time to take a look afresh at those things and to allow God to change that? Maybe it is.

...

If you are challenged by these words, turn to Appendix 2. Read the list carefully and prayerfully and ask God to show you those beliefs which do not line up with God's truth in His word.

Now write what God's word tells you about each belief you choose. Thank God for each truth eg Thank you Lord that you will never leave me…etc

Do this every day for the next month. As you do, allow Him to transform your mind and change your life.

Prayer:

Father, forgive me for the years I have lived my life in the bondage of ungodly beliefs. I have listed these before you. Thank you that you have shown me the truth of your word. Father, I ask you to help me from now on to live my life based on that truth. In Jesus' name, Amen.

The Truth about Ungodly Beliefs	
Romans 7:22 -23	I truly delight in God's commands, but it's pretty obvious that not all of me joins in that delight. Parts of me covertly rebel, and just when I least expect it, they take charge.
Romans 12:2	Don't become so well-adjusted to your culture that you fit into it without even thinking. Instead, fix your attention on God. You'll be changed from the inside out.
Ephesians 3:16a	I ask Him to strengthen you by His Spirit – not a brute strength but a glorious inner strength – that Christ will live in you as you open the door and invite Him in.
Colossians 3:2	Don't shuffle along, eyes to the ground, absorbed with the things right in front of you. Look up, and be alert to what is going on around Christ – that's where the action is. See things from His perspective.
Hebrews 8:10a-11	This time I'm writing out the plan in them, carving it on the lining of their hearts. I'll be their God, they'll be my people. They won't go to school to learn about me, or buy a book called God in Five Easy Lessons. They'll all get to know me firsthand, the little and the big, the small and the great.
1 Peter1:13	So roll up your sleeves, put your mind in gear, be totally ready to receive the gift that's coming when Jesus arrives.

Personal Notes:

The Seagull

Chapter 3

A Thursday Night in June
Christina's Story

Making choices

The girl who sat opposite me was 24 years old. Her name was Christina. I watched Christina across the room as she took a large sip of water and then set the glass back on the table noisily. Christina was about 5'5" in height and of medium build. She looked back at me with green eyes and grinned.

"Bet you've never heard a story like that?" she questioned triumphantly and took another drink.

I looked at her worn jeans and grey T-shirt thinking to myself as I did. I was so near and yet so far.

"Listen," I said as I mentally made a decision. "I'll make the appointment and I'll come with you so all you have to do is turn up."

"I've told you I'm no goin' to no doctors an' ye cannae make ma, so stop nippin' ma heed!" she said with a resolve that I knew that I had lost the battle for that day.

Still, I had also won some recently. Getting Christina to talk to me, even broaching the subject of some of the strange things she had been doing, was quite a victory to my mind.

So here I was on a cool November morning trying to encourage her to get help in a different sphere than we could offer. But Christina wasn't seeing any doctor and I knew that was the end of the conversation for the day.

Christina lived in the Barlanark area of Glasgow. We had visited her a few times and going there was not one of my favourite trips. Barlanark was one of the areas of the infamous ice-cream wars of the 1980's. By day ice-cream vans sold ice-cream but some vans stocked more than ice-cream. Stolen drink and cigarettes and sometimes drugs would often also be on sale. The story of the ice-cream wars has continued for over 20 years. Much value was placed on the turf of each ice-cream van and there were some honest owners who were hassled out of their area. One ice-cream man had been attacked twice in his van, fired on with a gun and beaten up outside his home. This tragedy ended with him and his family of six losing their life in a fire started in their home at night. All the appeals for information came to little as people knew that should they supply information to the police, their lives could be in danger.

In Christina's day, driving through Barlanark one could see tenement buildings boarded up with the odd light on, here and there, where people had not yet been decanted. Groups of men sat on street corners and small children played on the street till midnight. Still, outside other houses stood BMW's and Mercedes, no doubt the product of ill gotten gains.

Christina lived in a tenement block where most of the windows were still lit up at night. Their block had not been scheduled at that time for renovation or demolition, as had the other darkened blocks around the area.

Christina had an interesting heritage. It was 6000 BC that the Chinese people discovered that the "Camillus Satira" could be a source of fibre and food. It was in 1000AD that the Arabs discovered that the plant when dried could be smoked or eaten, to give you a wonderful sense of euphoria and well being. It was in 1990AD that Christina discovered this same stuff – hash – made her feel relaxed, that life in general seemed a little better and her sense of well-being increased. She could forget about her run down accommodation, mounting debt and intense loneliness and spend a few minutes feeling better.

We arrived at the Glasgow Elim Church in 1990 and Christina arrived a few months later. The church, being a Pentecostal church, had a good worship band led by an excellent worship leader. He was a prison officer by profession, from the east end of Glasgow. Al could certainly look after himself outside church, and inside too which was very necessary, as he was the man to spearhead modern contemporary worship in the church. When he said worship – you worshipped!

It was one Thursday evening that it happened. We had been involved in praise and worship for a while and the meeting was progressing nicely. I was playing the piano that evening, and we had just moved from *Celebrate, Jesus, Celebrate* down a beat or two into *There is a Redeemer, Jesus God's own Son.* The praise moved into worship to the sound of the triumphant hymn.

Christina, obviously very keen to be part of the proceedings, had been dancing and praising to the fast songs. But it now appeared that instead of slowing down along with the music, she was increasing time and tempo, faster and faster into what became a frenzied rave. I glanced at Kevin who was leading the meeting and watching her with some interest! He seemed content to let her be – that is until the gyrations began and her initial hops and leaps developed into what was more like a lap dance routine. By this time, Kevin had decided that lap dancing obviously wasn't on the menu for tonight and promptly began to search round for a deacon or leader to do the honours and persuade her of the same.

All the deacons having miraculously disappeared at that moment, he promptly decided he must face this one himself. Stepping boldly off the platform and beginning to walk towards the now transformed gyrating "blur" of movement accompanying *There is a Redeemer,* every eye moved for a second from the blur to watch the pastor progress down the aisle. I watched, as Kevin tapped the blur on what could have been a shoulder. The blur appeared to slow somewhat and then slow again until she transformed once more into a rather cross person interrupted in mid flight.

There appeared to be a few hurried exchanges followed by a few more and then Christina began to move again. It distinctly looked as though the blur was about to return, when Kevin spoke once more and both turned, headed for his office and disappeared through the door.

Once through the door, Christina went towards the end of the room and Kevin swiftly followed her inside.

"I want to speak to yous the noo," she shrieked.

Recognising at once that she had taken more than a cup of tea before she came to church that night and seeing the drug induced state in which she presented herself, Kevin spoke to her in a calm voice.

"Christina…" he began. But before he could say more, the tirade continued.

"Gauny shut up a minute? What is it wi you anyway? You'll no stop me!"

"You are not going back in there Christina," Kevin stated definitely, no doubt heart racing a little faster than he let on.

"You'll no' stop me. Touch me and I'll have you in Bar L," she repeated even louder than the first time and with those words, grabbed his tie which tightened round his neck. At once he took hold of her hands and released them from his tie pulling his tie loose and a couple of buttons from his shirt at the same time.

"You'll no' stop me," she shouted again and as she did, picked up a large metal chain belonging to the car park gate which had been removed earlier in the evening. With that, she began to menacingly swing it round in the air again and again.

"Christina," said Kevin, attempting to dodge the now whizzing chain as it flew past his left ear. "Put it down – you are not going back in."

This continued for a minute or so. Christina finding delight in her new toy and Kevin wondering firstly, where on earth were the deacons, and secondly, making a mental note that it would be a great idea for all pastors' offices to have a compulsory panic button installed for times exactly like these! As the chain was heavy, after ten rotations of the now slowing car park chain, the novelty was distinctly wearing off and the arm ache was overcoming the immediate need to behead the minister. Suddenly, Christina sat down on a nearby chair, and threw the offending object to the floor. Seizing his moment, Kevin grabbed it and with that, Christina flounced to the door, down the corridor and out into the street beyond.

Now, weeks later, here I was, face to face with Christina. Having made sure the car park chain was nowhere to be seen, I had led her into the pastor's office and we had talked for a while, around the issue of visiting the doctor. She had seemed to be off hash for a while and I knew that this choice could maybe change her life.

"C'mon, we'll go together," I said.

"Aye, that'll be right," Christina said sarcastically, as she looked at me with those piercing green eyes. "My choice is 'no'." I stared back at her knowing there was nothing I could say. Christina continued to come to church for a few more months and I, plus a few other people had similar conversations with her.

Two years later, in early December, we had not seen Christina for a long while. One afternoon a policeman knocked at the door of the church. He came to tell us that she had been found dead – she had been dead for six weeks and no one had noticed. No one knew whether it had been a deliberate drugs overdose or an accidental one. But they did know that she had been alone in a bed sit, and that no one had even noticed she'd not been around. We also knew that she was only 24 years old!

A few days later, we stood outside a Baptist church somewhere in the city. The funeral had been sad, but impersonal. Now groups of relatives stood around. Well spoken and even better dressed, they climbed into their Mercedes and 4x4's, bade farewell and drove away.

"Tragic," I said, locking up back at our own church that evening.

"If only…" replied Kevin as he fixed the chain on the car park gates and we walked to the car…

…

How do you rate the choices you have made in life? Life is about choices. We make choices from the moment we get up; to the moment we go to sleep. Some are big, some are small.

> Are there choices in your life that you wish you had never made? Choices that you have regretted or paid for severely? Or choices that you should have made but you didn't?
>
> Jesus stands before you right now to deal with those things once and for all. Why don't you tell Him of those mistakes and why don't you give Him the regret that you have carried for so long? He will take it from you and in return He will give you a peace to carry with you your whole life long, knowing those things are in His hands.
>
> Why don't you do that today?

Prayer:

Father God, my life is in your hands and you have seen me from the day I was conceived. You have seen my pathway and you have watched the choices I have made. Thank you for all the good choices in my life. I want to praise you for those Lord. (List them now before Him).

And yet, there have been times when my choices have not been wise ones and I want to lay these before you now. (Take time to tell Him about each one).

Father, I confess my wrong choices before you, times when I have strayed from what you would have me choose. I ask for your forgiveness today and from this time on, I ask you to guide me in a greater way. Let your still small voice direct me more and more in every choice I make. Thank you Lord. Amen.

"Be an arrow my child, aimed at my bull's eye. Search for wisdom, real wisdom, nothing you could wish for compares to wisdom to choose. It is for freedom that I have set you free. Choose again and again ways which will take you to

41

my freedom, my way. Allow my Holy Spirit to motivate all you do. Allow my Holy Spirit to fill you every day and to breathe life into your pathway until that day I choose to bring you home to me."

The Truth about your Choices	
Psalm 25:12	My question: What are God-worshippers like? Your answer: Arrows aimed at God's bull's eye.
Proverbs 8:10-11	Prefer my life-disciplines over chasing after money, and God-knowledge over a lucrative career. For wisdom is better than all the trappings of wealth; nothing you could wish for holds a candle to her.
Romans 6:16	You know well enough from your own experience that there are some acts of so-called freedom that destroy freedom. Offer yourselves to sin, for instance, and it's your last free act. But offer yourselves to the ways of God and the freedom never quits.
Galatians 5:16	My counsel is this: Live freely, animated and motivated by God's Spirit. Then you won't feed the compulsions of selfishness.
Galatians 5:17b-18	These two ways of life are antithetical, so that you cannot live at times one way and at times another way according to how you feel on any given day. Why don't you choose to be led by the Spirit and so escape the erratic compulsions of a law dominated-existence?
Philippians 1:9	So this is my prayer; that your love will flourish and that you will not only love much but well. Learn to love appropriately. You need to use your head and test your feelings so that your love is sincere and intelligent, not sentimental gush.

Personal Notes:

The Seagull

Chapter 4

The Golden Girls
The Seniors' Story

The power of words

I walked down the aisle to the front of the church and handed Kevin the note. The meeting was in full swing and the praise band was in top form that morning. Only recently had the transition been made from the traditional hymn prayer sandwich to the more modern form of worship, consisting of an extended time of worship songs beginning with lively praise and gradually transitioning over 30 minutes or so, to a more slow style of worship. Thankfully it had fallen to the previous pastor's lot to excellently negotiate that often turbulent transition. We were now able to enjoy the fruits of it.

I turned away from the platform and began to move towards the back of the church, and as I did my eye caught "the golden girls". One was sitting and two were standing, but all were doing their best to sing along with the new song for that morning. I knew later on, the hymn which would usually be included would be more to their taste but nevertheless I admired their willingness to be involved.

45

The golden girls consisted of Mrs McQuin, 75, Mrs McNaught aged 79 and Mrs Christie, a stately age of 87. They always sat on the third row from the front, centre block, right hand side.

Mrs McQuin had been brought to the church a decade ago by friends who still faithfully brought her each week, took her back and fed and watered her every Sunday lunchtime. Mrs Christie had arrived around twenty years ago, becoming an active participant and Mrs McNaught had been around some thirty years. All were extremely different but all sat in the same place and all worshipped the same God.

This was a week when Mrs McQuin's honorary family were away out of Glasgow and so at the end of the service, I carefully helped her into my black Fiat Uno and we started on the journey home. She was a very quiet lady but would usually have something to say when you were with her alone. Always words of encouragement, always words of hope.

"How's Joey?" I enquired, referring to the blue budgerigar who shared the flat with Mrs McQuin.

She lived in a tower block in the Gorbals which was not far from the church. The Gorbals, once a place of extreme poverty, tall crowded tenements and little daylight, now consisted of tower blocks and stand alone pubs which were left when the tenements were demolished.

"Fine," she replied, "Just fine."

"How's the lift?" I continued, remembering when she was marooned in her high flat for three days because the lifts were out of action and she was unable to negotiate the twenty plus flights of stairs up to her home.

The view from her window was stupendous. Looking to the north you could see the Kilpatrick Hills and the Campsie

Fells. Towards the west you could see out towards the Clyde Estuary.

I knew that the flat next door must have incredible views of the south out past Castlemilk and the forests beyond East Kilbride. Towards the east would be Livingston and Edinburgh.

Mrs McQuin had two sons. One son had passed away some months previously and the other one, she never saw. Never-the-less, her adopted family made sure with excellence that she had everything she needed.

"Thanks hen, it's been a good day," she said, as ten minutes later we ascended by a healthy lift to the 26th floor.

"Love to Joey," I said, as she unlocked the door of her flat and went inside.

Exactly one week later, I was pulling up by the kerbside in the Toryglen area of Glasgow. It was Sunday once again and it was my custom each Sunday morning, to stop on the way from Croftfoot to Govanhill to pick up Mrs McNaught. Mrs McNaught was a colourful character and this morning was no different from the rest. She had two passions and she had two hates. The first of her passions was Robbie Burns and every Sunday morning without fail before very long, she would be quoting:

"O wad some power the giftie gie us (O would some power the gift to give us),
To see oursels as ithers see us! (To see ourselves as others see us),
It wad frae monie a blunder free us, (It would from many a 'blunder' free us),
An' foolish notion: (And foolish notion),
What airs in dress an' gait wad lea'e us, (What airs in dress and gait would leave us),

An' ev'n devotion!" (and even devotion!)

Sunday by Sunday the quotation would come until I could almost recite it myself. Robert Burns was a poet and writer of traditional Scottish poems and songs. His works are famous throughout the world and even though he died in 1796, he has millions of fans. Mrs McNaught was one of them. In fact, it was as if Mrs McNaught was a personal friend of his!

I pulled up by the pavement outside the Catholic church where she always waited.

"You're late," she said, as she climbed in wearing her usual fur coat and pearls. "I was up to high doh wondering where you were!"

"I put some washing out Duchess," I said as she slammed the door shut.

"Never mind, don't knock yer pan in for me," she replied.

We always called her the Duchess. Clad in furs and pearls she always looked perfect. A widow for several years with one son living outside Glasgow, she now lived in Toryglen which was maybe something of a come down to more affluent days. Mrs McNaught had met Jesus when she was 24 years old at a George Jeffreys' Crusade in Glasgow. George Jeffreys was a Welsh man who was baptised in the Holy Spirit in 1910 in Sunderland and became the leader of the Elim denomination from its commencement, until he split with it around 1940. He spent many years running crusades through Britain and left many churches in his wake.

George Jeffreys was Mrs McNaught's second passion. I distinctly remember Kevin inviting her onto the platform one Sunday morning to share how she met God.

"I was saved during a visit of Principal George Jeffreys," she began. And then she paused thoughtfully. Then looking at

Kevin she said, "Our pastor does his best, but George Jeffreys, he *was* a man of God!"

But that was Mrs McNaught. She said it as she saw it and she gave us many an amusing moment in doing so.

Mrs McNaught also had two pet hates. One was loud praise music, and she would mutter away long after the worship band had stopped and the second was music being played during the communion part of the service. As the bread and wine were being passed from person to person often the pianist would begin to play quiet music in the background. Several times Mrs McNaught shouted, "Gauny shut up...shut up..." to him as he played. But people just smiled and loved her all the more. That was just The Duchess!

The last of the golden girls but by no means the least, was Mrs Christie. I remember my first contact with Mrs Christie was on our first Sunday at the church. She walked up to me at the end of the service, thrust out her hand and said, "Hello, are you new here?"

"Yes, I am," I replied, "I'm your new pastor's wife."

"Oh my goodness," she looked shocked. "Please forgive me, I thought you were one of the teenagers!"

I always liked her from then on!

A couple of weeks later, we met in the corridor and she came up to me and said, "I hope you don't mind me asking, but what would you like me to call you?"

"Call me Margaret," I replied, and then continued, "And what would you like me to call you?" expecting her to say call me Janie or something.

"You can call me Mrs Christie, good to have you here," she said and she disappeared into the crowd.

Over the first few days and weeks of our new life in the church, I found Scotland to be very different and I found Glasgow to be even more different than all that I was familiar with. It seemed that everything had changed. My home had changed, my church had changed, my career had gone, my friends were 300 miles away, the accents had changed – I couldn't understand what people said. I remember needing to get the car taxed the first week after our move and had to fetch Kevin into the post office to understand where the main post office was. He couldn't understand the post office assistant's strong Glaswegian accent either and in the end we asked the poor man to write it down!

On the other hand, the cupboards had been filled with food and people popped by to see how we were doing. Our church could not have been kinder, but I still found those early days a stretching experience. The streets full of flats and the high tenement buildings, the boarded up windows of the then Castlemilk were so different from where we had lived and the culture shock was big.

One sunny Wednesday afternoon we arranged to go for tea at the home of Mrs Christie who lived out of the city. We travelled out of our area, up towards her home. Suddenly, I was seeing things which were familiar to me and later as we sat in her beautifully old fashioned room sipping tea and eating sandwiches, watching the leafy trees in the long garden sway in the breeze, for the first time, I knew it was going to be okay.

Mrs Christie was definitely a fully paid up member of the Glasgow Church. Many a time, I would pull up outside her home at 3am or even 6am and unload this sprightly old lady who had joined us in our half night or all night of prayer. In her eighties, she may have been but she wasn't going to miss out on what God was doing. What her family, with whom she lived, thought about her rolling in at 6am, I have no idea.

Mrs Christie was the epitome of encouragement. During sermons, she would be agreeing, nodding and encouraging all the way through. Whatever the subject she was with you – she was really on the cutting edge of the church in those days.

There was one Sunday when Kevin had just finished his sermon; the subject for the morning was "The Value of Virginity." Mrs Christie had listened with rapt attention through all ten points. At the end of the service as Kevin came off the platform, she immediately hobbled towards him at the front.

"Pastor, can I have a word with you?" she asked, reaching his side.

"Certainly," said Kevin, thinking that perhaps, this time, it was a subject too far for Mrs Christie.

She looked Kevin straight in the eyes and said, "Thank you so much for that wonderful sermon…I *really* needed to hear that." And with those words she left the building! She was 88 at the time!

As I sit writing these words, all three wonderful ladies have long transferred to the big church in the sky. Had you walked into our church then, you would not have given them a second glance and yet the power they held in their words was immense. At a time in life when they no doubt wished for stability and status quo, in their own way, they were willing to stay on the cutting edge for God. They had no idea of the power of their words to help us in those first few years – or maybe they did – who knows?

...

What are the words you speak every day? Words to family, or friends, colleagues or strangers? Are they words of life, or words of death? In several surveys done recently, it was discovered that 50 per cent of all vocabulary used to express emotion was negative, 30 per cent was positive and 20 per cent was neutral. Every age, gender and cultural group had the same proportions, 50, 30 and 20.

And what about the words which have been spoken **over** you?

The power of words has been so great in your life. There have been billions of words spoken to you and about you. Some positive, some negative and these words can affect what you think and feel and do, years after they have been spoken.

Your Father in heaven has heard every word, the good and the bad and He chooses today to release you from the effects of the negative, and speak His own words of life to your spirit. Why don't you let Him do that?

Look down the two lists below.
Consider which words are part of your vocabulary.
Begin to allow God to transform your words to words of life.

Positive words/feelings
Love, like, good, better, happy, great, care, excited, patient, strong, cheerful, good, friendly, relaxed, comfortable, proud, thankful, grateful, admire, inspire, secure, content, amazed, awe, important, appreciate, delighted, peaceful, attractive,

beautiful, enthusiastic, eager, warm, optimistic, interested, amused, brave, hope, glad, brilliant.

Negative words/feelings
Ashamed, criticize, I don't, I can't, I won't, embarrassed, humiliate, inferior, ugly, insulted, mocked, offended, resentful, ridicule, inhibited, manipulated, controlled, trapped, abandoned, alone, confused, disapprove, discouraged, lonely, accused, judged, misled, punished, abused, afraid, frightened, intimidated, scared, suspicious.

Prayer:
Father, I examine the words I use every day. Please forgive me when I speak negative things to people or about people in my life. I choose today to ask you to erase these from my vocabulary. Would you begin to make me someone who spreads life with the words I speak. I want to bring life to people around. Life to their confidence, sense of well being and esteem. Life to their motivation, desire and dreams. Help me, Lord, from this day on, to be a life giver.
In Jesus' name, Amen.

The Truth about the Power of Words	
Proverbs 12:18	Rash language cuts and maims, but there is healing in the words of the wise.
Proverbs 13:17	Irresponsible talk makes a real mess of things, but a reliable reporter is a healing presence.
Proverbs 15:4	Kind words heal and help; cutting words wound and maim.
Proverbs 15:23	Congenial conversation – what a pleasure! The right word at the right time – beautiful!
Proverbs 16:24	Gracious speech is like clover honey – good taste to the soul, quick energy for the body.
Ecclesiastes 5:2	Don't shoot off your mouth, or speak before you think. Don't be too quick to tell God what you think He wants to hear. God's in charge, not you – the less you speak, the better.
Matthew 15:11	It's not what enters one's mouth that defiles a person but what comes out of one's mouth.

Personal Notes:

The Seagull

Chapter 5

That Was The Week That Was
A Street's Story

Generational influences

I looked at the parcel on the desk. It was round and wrapped in green paper. I walked over to the desk and put it in my bag then I turned and left the office, closing the door behind me.

There were very few Sunday mornings in those early days that I didn't leave the church each week with one or more little gifts left on Kevin's desk for us to take home. A pot of jam, a card, a home made bookmark, a stick of rock, the presents were wide and varied but we appreciated them all.

One of the overriding characteristics of Glasgow life we found was the culture of giving. From those with much to those with nothing, hospitality was the name of the game. After three months in that city and an increasing waistline, we decided to dispense with planning our visits ahead of time, as many pre-arranged visits constituted a cooked meal prepared for our arrival. The first one of the day was fine but by the third or fourth meal, we were feeling remarkably like something between Billy Bunter and the Vicar of Dibley. I remember on the first visit to the city Kevin had travelled on to the north of Scotland for a speaking engagement and I had stayed behind to travel back to Derby the next day. At five o'clock I was served rolls, cakes, biscuits and savouries. I ate my fill believing that I had to last until the next morning before having anything further to eat. At five thirty, the hostess began preparing the evening meal of a three course dinner. What I had just eaten was mid afternoon snack!

Anyone who has visited Scotland will know that "D'you fancy a wee cup a tea?" means, "Would you like a cup of tea, a plate of biscuits, maybe cake and often a sandwich too?" A drink is never served without an accompanying snack.

On one occasion, new to the city, we asked directions. "Sorry I cannae help yous," the man replied, "But have a sweet instead."

On another, we had recently decided to begin to save for a trip aboard and the next morning we found a huge whisky bottle half full of loose change to go towards the cost of our trip.

On yet another occasion, we found out that Sharon, one of our members had had her electricity cut off because she had put all her money into a special offering for our church extension. There are hundreds of examples of the generosity of the Glaswegian culture.

And yet running parallel to the many amazing attributes of this city, there run some strands which have evolved for generations and hold many in their grip. Children are born into these things and learn them as the tools of their trade. It is in their DNA, it is part of their make up.

We had recently begun a new Watchman Intercession group in the church, members would individually pray every day and then meet together once a month. The meetings were powerful and no one wanted to miss these amazing times.

Sometimes we would travel out in cars to different points of the city to pray or simply to listen to God and then return to the building to intercede for the area.

It was on a Tuesday afternoon that Kevin's associate pastor returned to the church. He drove down the street and swung round the side of the building into the church car park. Securing his car steering lock he opened the door and got out of the car. He then began to walk back towards the front door of the church but as he did he heard a noise coming from the back of the church. It was a muffled sound and not too noisy. Puzzled, he turned to investigate. On rounding the corner, he looked down and saw the couple. A local prostitute had set up her business for the afternoon in the church car park. Derek had a dilemma, should he interrupt the passion and send them packing, facing possibly a chibbing or even worse, a stabbing? Or should he discreetly leave the scene retreating to the safety of the building. Wisely, discretion became the better part of valour and he turned and crept into the building, returning to the window to check on them regularly!

It was a couple of days later when the phone rang and a voice said, "You'd better come down to the church the noo, Pastor." It was the janny.

"Some bampot's been at it alright…there's blood all over the doors and windows," he continued.

Kevin got in the car and travelled down to Inglefield Street to see blood smeared over the main doors, the window and step. As John, our janitor, showed him round, he saw there was blood on several of the windows. Was this some obscure ritual of witchcraft, or did it symbolise something else? After finding nothing else, he was just beginning to help the janny start to clear up when someone came out of the hostel opposite.

The Seagull

"There was a bad fight in the night over the bridge and I saw a wee guy injured...chappin' on the church door so he was," he said. "We saw what was happening and called the police," he said, "and they did the rest."

Violence is still very active in certain areas of the city. Gang warfare accounts for much of this violence. For the teenage gangs, fighting is part of the gang culture and for the more mature, sophisticated gangs deal in drugs, money lending and protection rackets.

We finished clearing up and as we did, my mind went back briefly to a particular morning when we had been unable to come out of the church due to a fight between two gangs which were positioned either side of the bridge close to the church. They were throwing home made Molotov cocktails at each other! It certainly livened up our morning prayer time!

And so we came to the Tuesday of that week, when someone came into the church, having parked their car in the car park at the side. Walking round the front of the building, they saw something sticking out of the grass and on bending down, discovered two syringes, hidden in the grass. Knowing the hostel to have a safe box, we enlisted their help. We had called on them before when an addict sadly locked himself in the loo before shooting up into his groin and collapsing. That particular night, we ended up breaking the door down to get him out. Following that incident anyone who went into the loo with a carrier bag became highly suspicious, including the deacons!

On the Saturday we arrived at the church to find cassette tape across the road and wound round the fence. This is a practice sometimes used by witches in many areas.

Witchcraft is prevalent in the city. On one occasion, while walking our dog up on the high ground near Castlemilk, suddenly he became highly agitated and was totally uncontrollable. Eventually we managed to retrieve and reprimand him. Later we found that that area is used for witchcraft rituals on certain days of the year. We didn't recognize it, but the dog did!

Just four pictures in a week: sex, violence, drugs and witchcraft. Just a few examples of many more things which hold people captive in Glasgow and in many other cities in Britain.

The next day was Sunday and as I looked round that morning I saw those who had been set free from these things. Gina, a prostitute for 30 years and Shaz, also a prostitute for many years now involved in the freedom of others. Many who had served a prison sentence now radically saved. Jeff served a prison sentence for fire bombing a property, also slashed in Balinnee, Sean in prison for violence, Emily, a victim of severe physical abuse, Rab, physically abused, Bert, violent to his children. Si, on heroin for many years, Mike, an AIDS sufferer who brought his friend to church and cared for him until he died and Bev, into witchcraft who spent years getting free from its effects.

All products of their past, and yet Jesus came to set them free, physically, mentally, emotionally and spiritually. It was for freedom that Christ came to liberate them and not just those above, but the thousands which each one symbolises.

We prayed with renewed vigour at the Watchman meeting the next week.

...

Are there things in your family which are patterns or trends?

Trends of sin (spiritual) or rejection (emotional) or illness (physical) or fear (mental)? We inherit from our parents and those who have gone before us, through example, through genes and through many other ways.

It is for freedom that Christ has set you free and it is that cross which has the power to break the power of sin in your life and to bring blessing to your experience. We are responsible for our own lives, even though we are influenced by our generational forefathers.

Why don't you allow God to set you free from the past and to bless your life in a new way today?

...

Prayer:

Father, thank you that it is for freedom that you set me free, when you died on the cross. Today, I want to appropriate the power of that cross to every part of my life – the past, the present and the future.

I lay before you the effects of my forfathers on my life, both the good and the bad:

- *all I have physically inherited*
- *all modelling which has influenced my mind*
- *all the sin which has affected me spiritually*

- *all the actions which have wounded me emotionally*

I place the cross of Jesus between myself and all these things and I thank you that as I do, I make a choice to live out of that freedom which your cross provides for me.
In Jesus' name, Amen.

Now take time to read aloud God's list of blessings over your life and the life of your family.

If you fully obey the Lord your God and carefully follow all His commands I give you today, the Lord your God will set you high above all the nations on earth.

All these blessings will come upon you and accompany you if you obey the Lord your God:

You will be blessed in the city and blessed in the country.

The fruit of your womb will be blessed, and the crops of your land and the young of your livestock – the calves of your herds and the lambs of your flocks.

Your basket and your kneading trough will be blessed.

You will be blessed when you come in and blessed when you go out.

The Lord will grant that the enemies who rise up against you will be defeated before you. They will come at you from one direction but flee from you in seven.

The Lord will send a blessing on your barns and on everything you put your hand to. The Lord your God will bless you in the land He is giving you.

The Lord will establish you as His holy people, as He promised you on oath, if you keep the commands of the Lord your God and walk in His ways.

Then all the peoples on earth will see that you are called by the name of the Lord, and they will fear you.

The Lord will grant you abundant prosperity – in the fruit of your womb, the young of your livestock and the crops of your ground – in the land He swore to your forefathers to give you.

The Lord will open the heavens, the storehouse of His bounty, to send rain on your land in season and to bless all the work of your hands. You will lend to many nations but will borrow from none.

The Lord will make you the head, not the tail. If you pay attention to the commands of the Lord your God that I give you this day and carefully follow them, you will always be at the top, never at the bottom.

Do not turn aside from any of the commands I give you today, to the right or to the left, following other gods and serving them.

Deuteronomy 28:1-14

The Truth about Generational Influences	
Proverbs 11:29	Exploit or abuse your family, and end up with a fistful of air; common sense tells you it's a stupid way to live.
Psalm 102:28	Your servants' children will have a good place to live and their children will be at home with you.
Psalm 103:17	God's love, though, is ever and always, eternally present to all who fear Him, making everything right for them and their children as they follow His Covenant ways and remember to do whatever He said.
Psalm 112:1-2	Hallelujah! Blessed man, blessed woman, who fear God, who cherish and relish His commandments. Their children robust on the earth, and the homes of the upright – how blessed!
Proverbs 13:22a	A good life gets passed on to the grandchildren.
Isaiah 44:3b-4	I will pour my Spirit into your descendants and my blessing on your children. They shall sprout like grass on the prairie, like willows alongside creeks.
Deuteronomy 5:9b-10	I hold parents responsible for any sins they pass on to their children to the third and yes, even to the fourth generation. But I'm lovingly loyal to the thousands who love me and keep my commandments.

Personal Notes:

Chapter 6

Angels and Things
A Holy Spirit Story

Putting God in a box

"...I will come to you in a thick cloud, Moses, so the people themselves can hear me when I speak to you..." Exodus 19:9.

I read the few verses from the Bible, eating toast as I did. We had just been on our morning walk around the golf course behind our house – the dog and I. The golf course lay on a steep slope at the top of which stood our home. Each morning Mary and I enjoyed the cool stillness of the morning, as we made our way round the outer edge of the golf course, listening to the dull drone of the morning rush into the city of Glasgow.

Now, back in the house, sharing a couple of slices of toast, we sat in front of the floor-to-ceiling window looking out onto the awakening city beyond the green course and the Campsie Fells beyond.

Contemplating whether to eat the last piece of toast myself, or pass it in the direction of the hopeful eyes beside me, I looked up from the few verses I had been reading. As I did, something caught my eye. I popped the last piece of toast into my mouth and walked to the window. A disappointed dog followed me. As I looked, a thick cloud was swirling around the window. I looked down at my Bible. I looked again at the window. I began to read on.

"...go down and prepare the people. Consecrate them today and tomorrow...be sure they are ready for the third day for on that day the Lord will come down..." Exodus 19:10.

"I don't know how long 'today and tomorrow' are, a day, a week a month, I don't know...but I think it's significant," I said to Kevin later.

"Something could be on the way," Kevin replied.

God was to give us that passage a few times in our ministry at Glasgow, but that was the first time.

"Today and tomorrow" turned out to be the next two seasons. We had always divided our year up into three parts, January to April, May to August and September to December, so we set to work preparing the church through the autumn period and then through spring. Starting in May 1994, we were to experience some amazing phenomena of the power and presence of God on an ongoing basis.

May 1994 dawned and soon after that, the power of God began to fall in a new way. It was common for people to go to the front of the church each week at the end of a service. Some of them would stand to be prayed for and on occasions some would fall to the ground under the power of the Holy Spirit. But suddenly this was not confined to meetings.

On one occasion, we had just returned from a conference in Sunderland where we had both been greatly impacted by the Holy Spirit. We opened the outer door of the church and inside just leaving the building was Si, one of our guitarists. Si had been a heroin user for some years. He had been miraculously healed of hepatitis following his conversion. He was now drug free, on fire for God and a member of our praise band.

"Hi," he said as we came face to face in the foyer. "Just back from the conference?" "Whoa!" he suddenly exclaimed, as he started to overbalance backwards as if some invisible force were pushing him.

"We must have brought back plenty of the Holy Spirit," Kevin replied as he waved his arm towards Si.

The presence of God suddenly fell all around us and Si ended upon the floor. We enjoyed praying for him for quite a while.

But it was not confined to inside the building. During a period of nightly meetings when the power of God was very strong upon the proceedings, people testified to getting out of their cars and being slain in the Spirit in the car park.

It was a Sunday morning in November when we had these phenomena during communion. Being from a Brethren church originally, communion has always had a very special place in our hearts and in our conviction and communion took place in our church, rain or shine, every week. The service had been very powerful, ministry in prayer had already taken place and several people were still lying on the floor enjoying the strong presence of God upon them. Being time for the communion, Kevin gestured a suitable song to the worship leaders and called the four servers to the front. The first one to arrive there reached within four feet of the table and promptly fell to the floor under the power of God. One by one the other three did the same. Kevin, looking a little amused, looked around and then signalled to four more people to come forward to serve the bread and the wine. The same thing happened to the next four also. Looking round for the four most backslidden people in the church – he then decided that maybe God had a different agenda and that Sunday we enjoyed a very reverent, meaningful evening communion.

On another occasion there was a line of people standing waiting for prayer. The atmosphere was incredible and suddenly as I sat at the piano I saw the whole line of people fall virtually at the same time. Frank, who was at the keyboard on the stage, mouthed over to Kevin.

"Did you feel that?" he asked.

"Feel what?" said Kevin.

"Feel the wind – just before they fell?" he said.

Many of those in the prayer line testified to the same thing. People sat and laughed for hours, one person testified that she had never had a father and felt that her Father God had picked her up and was bouncing her on his knee – that's why she was laughing and giggling. That was a very healing moment for her. Some who shook right through the meeting testified that they felt God was shaking out things that they had held onto for years and years and that they felt free and more alive than ever before.

I had visited an elderly lady who was no longer able to attend the church. Upon leaving I had taken her hands and prayed for her. At the end of the prayer, she said, "As you prayed, I felt electricity going right up my arms and all round by body and I feel the most glorious presence of God ever." After that every time I saw her, she always spoke of the occasion when she felt the power of God in a tangible way.

Time and time again these things kept happening. On another occasion, the chairs were at the side of the room and people were standing, kneeling and lying in various places right throughout the sanctuary. Several young adults, who by the looks on their faces were obviously un-churched, came in to watch what was going on. They stood for a while, and then one volunteered to receive prayer. Halfway through the prayer he stopped the person praying to say he could smell the most amazing fragrance all around him. Often in the church, the familiar musky fragrance could be smelled though on that occasion, the prayee had no prior knowledge of this experience.

During the same period in a morning seminar, the speaker was explaining that the time is coming when people will come in off the street and ask to be saved. A little while later in the same meeting, someone actually walked into the meeting. "I've been thinking about getting my life sorted," said the man, "And I just passed this church so I thought I'd do it today."

It was an amazing morning when the congregation, listening to a sermon about Elisha and the floating axe head, saw the shape of an axe being slowly but clearly formed on the ceiling above the pastor. This was made by the rays of the sun shining in a certain way through the window but it was so distinct and clear and it caused so much stir amongst the watching congregation that Kevin stopped his sermon to ask what everyone was talking about.

Probably one of the most memorable occasions was involving Brian. Brian was a draughtsman and a regular part of our church. In the church, we had two types of people. There were those we called the "feelers", those who physically could feel the presence of God, and also there were the "thinkers", those who responded best by thinking through what was taking place and walking more in faith on their journey. Both of these groups were valuable to our church life and progress. Although Brian enjoyed the things of the Spirit, he was a thinker more than a feeler, that is to say he liked to watch and work things out first. He could appreciate others being

71

touched by physical manifestations but didn't really share in them himself.

It was one Sunday morning when Kevin began to experience a strong feeling of the weight of God when he was preaching. He continued to preach, standing up straight, then bending forward as he felt that weight. Suddenly the draughtsman got up and hurriedly left the room. We were worried that he was upset by what was happening on the platform. Kevin continued to preach and I followed Brian into the corridor.

"Are you OK?" I asked.

"No, I'm not," he replied.

Oh dear, I thought, so I asked, "What's wrong?"

"I'm not going back in there," replied Brian.

"Is it because of Kevin?" I said.

"No," he replied. "It's because of that eight foot angel standing behind him who keeps tapping him on the head!"

Exciting times, witnessed by many. Physical manifestations of the intervention of God in human lives.

We are living in amazing times where God is sweeping through many churches with His presence, when both churched and un-churched are able to witness the manifest presence of God in physical, emotional and spiritual healings. We say "more, Lord," not just in the buildings but outside too and everywhere His people go.

*See Appendix 1 for other accounts of the above events.

...

It's amazing how often we try to put God in a box. We expect God to fit into our expectations – because it feels safe. We like to stay within our comfort zone and we forget the supernatural experiences of the Bible.

God has moved in times gone by in awesome ways, and He moves today. Do you long for a greater thirst to see His power manifest in this world? Let Him bring that about in you.

Prayer:

Father, as I come to you, I pray that you will begin to amaze me. Forgive me for my tunneled vision which prevents you from showing me your true glory. Forgive me when I reject what I do not understand, simply because I have no framework for it. I acknowledge your supernatural works of bible times. I acknowledge all you are doing around the world and I acknowledge your mighty hand at work in our land today. Help me to know that you have my best at heart. You are a mighty God and I look to see more of your mighty power at work.
In Jesus' name, Amen.

Now spend some time listening to some quiet music and allow Him to do His amazing work in you, so He can take you to higher heights and deeper depths in Him.

The Truth about God's Power	
2 Kings 6:17	Then Elisha prayed, "O God, open his eyes and let him see." The eyes of the young man were opened and he saw. A wonder! The whole mountainside full of horses and chariots of fire surrounding Elisha!
Daniel 5:5-6a	At that very moment, the fingers of a human hand appeared and began writing on the lamp-illuminated, whitewashed wall of the palace. When the king saw the disembodied hand writing away, he went white as a ghost.
Luke 24:4b	Then, out of nowhere it seemed, two men, light cascading over them, stood there.
Acts 2:2	Without warning there was a sound like a strong wind, gale force, no one could tell where it came from.
Acts 5:15	They even carried the sick out into the streets and laid them on stretchers and bedrolls, hoping they would be touched by Peter's shadow when he walked by.
Acts 9:3-4	When he got to the outskirts of Damascus, he was suddenly dazed by a blinding flash of light. As he fell to the ground, he heard a voice, "Saul, Saul, why are you out to get me?"

Personal Notes:

The Seagull

Chapter 7

Distant Drums
Joan's Story

The place of mercy

"Arrgh..."

I looked across the aircraft as the plane fell several feet in the sky. There were two very scared people three rows back. Stuart and Ann had been nicely nodding off on flight 724 when, suddenly, the plane begun to shudder and it fell some feet in the sky before continuing on its course.

"A wind pocket I expect," I thought and continued my conversation. As I did, I looked across the cabin and my eyes scanned the sixty-two people we had brought on this trip to Canada. A variety of ages and experiences were on the journey with us and for many, it was their first flight. Some of them were to come several times overseas with us but this was our first organised trip.

Glasgow is a city of mixed ages and experiences. As with most cities it is usually the more affluent people who get to travel and so in some parts of Glasgow, some may be born, live and die within the same area, never having travelled much further.

I was glad that we were at least off the ground. As I looked around the cabin, some of the new flyers were rising to the challenge admirably, and some still looked rather pensive. One person nearly hadn't made it through departures. We had sat with Isabel in the booking hall as all our people checked in. She had never flown or been abroad, and she found this moment just too difficult to overcome. Putting the money aside week by week had been easy by comparison. Attending the instructions meeting was a little scarier, but this was something else – flying 3,000 miles to Canada suddenly seemed impossible and no matter how much we talked, Isabel stayed glued to her seat.

But once we were through to the departure lounge, the excitement took over and everyone else made it safely through onto the aircraft and into the air, not without a few screams and yells from one or two on take off, I hasten to add, but that just added to the fun.

My eyes continued to scan the plane and eventually came to rest on Joan. She sat on the end seat near to the aisle, all strapped in safely, not missing one moment of the experience.

Joan had met and married her husband when she was very young and in a matter of months the twosome became a threesome. Les worked as a tradesman and brought in a steady wage for the little family. Their tenement flat was beautifully kept by Joan and well provided for by Les, but it often seemed that more than a few pounds began to go the way of the bevvie. Les's local public house was situated in the Govan area of Glasgow not too far from his house. Les enjoyed the atmosphere in that place. There was fun and laughs and the drink flowed.

From the outside, the pubs in Glasgow looked run down. Open all day and some of the night, long before England adopted the longer drinking laws, some men would arrive first thing in a morning and stay till last thing at night when they would be helped home by friends or left to rest on the pavement. Some pubs would be painted blue and some green and there were certain ones which if we went in as English, it's doubtful we would come out in one piece. Some pubs took regular collections for the IRA and some were simply ordinary corner pubs. In other areas, it was strange to see every inch of the place demolished, yet the pub left standing.

All too suddenly, violence could erupt out of nothing at all. It was all too easy during a dispute for a heated party to smash a bottle and chib the nearest face around. Many of the marks on faces around Glasgow have been caused in a pub brawl.

These pubs were a delight to many a man in Glasgow during that time, but a horror to many a wife who waited in fear for the sound of the door opening in the early hours of the morning.

Often as people came to church and committed their lives to God, they would bring their bottles of alcohol to Kevin and rather than leave them about his office, he would store them in the cupboard. Unfortunately the gas meter was also in that cupboard. One morning there was a tap on his door and in walked the gas man to read the meter.

"How's it gaun, Da?" he said with a big smile on his face.

"Help yourself, it's in there," said Kevin, forgetting about all the booze in there too. The gas man took the reading then stood back, eyeing all the bottles and said, "This for when the sermon preparation gets a bit tough, Pastor?" with a twinkle in his eye.

"Oh dear – it's not mine," Kevin replied earnestly.

"That'll be right. Sure it's not..." said the gas man, his grin getting wider.

"Have a nice day," he concluded with a wink and a grin and left the office.

For Les, the drink that he kept in the cupboard at home was his, but it all seemed harmless. For him, a game of pool after work, a few bevvies provided good relaxation, but as time went on, an hour turned into two and then three and then four until Joan became that wife who waited for the sound of the door opening late into the night.

I looked again around the aircraft, many were dozing. Some had tuned into the film and some were still chatting excitedly. One or two were still looking pensively out of the window as though willing the plane to stay in the sky. I noticed at the back, Rab was standing in conversation with two air hostesses. His easy Glaswegian patter and his quick sense of humour working its way as usual into their hearts. Maggie was deep in conversation with a stranger across the aisle and Joan likewise. I looked back at Joan and thought how different this was from her life back at home.

Nowadays Les, house bound with the effects of alcohol, spent his days and nights in a world that would never change. The evenings at the Old Man Pub had transformed into the need for more and more of the whisky which over time stole his job, his health and would tragically, eventually steal his life.

Nevertheless, a trip to visit him was always a good experience. Les always sat in the same chair now, needing his daily dose of whisky which would prevent the detox symptoms coming upon him with vengeance.

"Coffee, Pastor?" asked Joan, as Kevin sat down in the beautifully laid out lounge.

"He disnae like coffee," retorted Les, "You might think a'm away with the fairies but I know he disnae like coffee!"

And then to Kevin, "How's it goin' big un?"

"Seen any good films lately?" Kevin would say and the conversation revolved round Hollywood and things of a bygone era. Les loved singing and the visit would invariably end up with the strains of *I was born under a wandering star* and *I hear the sound of distant drums* coming from the tenement flat in Govan.

Joan always lived to a set routine. She would rise early in the morning, to her job, being back in time to aid her husband with washing and showering. Out to shop then back for lunch. Jobs in the afternoon then back to cook for dinner. When church meetings were on, Joan would be there but careful not to leave her husband alone too long. God had joined them together and in sickness and in health we watched her faithfulness.

It was a dream to watch her tread those aircraft steps onto the tarmac, to check into the hotel. It was a dream to watch her live the week, laughing and even crying at times, to see God renewing her youth again. To see the difference in a week, what an amazing week! But these things do come to an end and we soon arrived back in Glasgow.

Days turned into weeks and weeks turned into months and there came a day when my birthday card no longer said from Joan and Les, simply from Joan. One cold November night Les heard the sound of distant drums himself and passed away at the age of 52. Caught like thousands around him in the net of alcoholism yet he always had a song to the end.

Everyone has a story. And Joan has a story too. She had a choice to make in the situation in which she found herself. A choice of mercy or a choice of judgement. She could not change her situation but she could stand, as best she could, in the place of mercy or she could walk everyday in judgement. But she knew, in hers and in every situation, mercy triumphs over judgement. And day after day, she chose mercy.

...

Will you stand in the place of mercy or will you stand in the place of judgment?

The place of judgement is the enemy's ground and when we stand in this place, the enemy has legal rights to affect our lives.

The place of mercy is God's ground and it is in this place that the enemy loses his right to claim on our lives.

Jesus says if you forgive, you will be forgiven. Choose today to stand in the place of mercy towards those who wrong you, and allow God's mercy and blessing to shower down on your life in a new way.

Mercy triumphs over judgement.

...

List those in your life who you hold in the place of mercy, who have wronged you and you have truly forgiven.

Now list those in your life who you still hold in the place of judgement.

Ask God to work in your heart and give you grace to forgive, to give them a gift they maybe don't deserve and to move on.

Prayer:

Father God, I thank you for your hand upon my life and I thank you for the place I have in you. Thank you for the mercy you continue to pour down over my life every day. Father, help me to stay in that place of mercy, that place where the enemy has no rights to claim on my life. Forgive me when I move to the place of judgement, where the enemy has legal right to affect my life. Lord, you have said, "If I judge, I will be judged and if I forgive I will be forgiven."

I now make a choice, Lord, to move from that place of judgement to the place of mercy and to seek to live in that place afresh every day, from this time on.
In Jesus' name, Amen.

The Truth about Mercy over Judgement	
Micah 6:8	But He's already made it plain how to live, what to do, what God is looking for in men and women. It's quite simple: Do what is fair and just to your neighbour, be compassionate and loyal in your love, and don't take yourself too seriously – take God seriously.
Matthew 5:7	You're blessed when you care. At the moment of being "care-full", you find yourselves cared for.
Matthew 7:3-4	It's easy to see a smudge on your neighbour's face and be oblivious to the ugly sneer on your own. Do you have the nerve to say, "Let me wash your face for you," when your own face is distorted by contempt?
Matthew 18:32-33	The king summoned the man and said, "You evil servant! I forgave your entire debt when you begged me for mercy. Shouldn't you be compelled to be merciful to your fellow servant who asked for mercy?"
Luke 6:37	Do not judge, and you will not be judged. Do not condemn, and you will not be condemned. Forgive, and you will be forgiven.
James 2:13	For if you refuse to act kindly, you can hardly expect to be treated kindly. Kind mercy wins over harsh judgment every time.

Personal Notes:

The Seagull

Chapter 8

The Great Physician
Annie's Story

The power of soaking

I stood and waited on the path, watching as the group of teenagers passed by. No one looked my way or heeded in any way, myself or the dog which stood by my side. Suddenly, the door behind me opened and I swung round to see Mitch with a wide grin on his face, not at me, but at my dog, Mary.

"In ya come," he said in a broad Glaswegian dialect. I walked up the two steps into the small house in Govan.

"I widna think there wis much you could dae," he said as he closed the door, finishing his conversation with a bodyless voice from the kitchen.

"Wishing's nae use and ah'm no caring anyway," he continued, as he led us through the door and then he turned to Mary.

"Ah'm com' tae ye. Ah'm comin…come to ye Da for a wee clap…"

I followed Mitch into the kitchen to find a blonde haired woman around thirty years of age, sitting at the kitchen table.

"I've got some papers for the house group," I said as I sat down across from Annie.

"I'm just after my tea," she said and motioned to the chair opposite.

We passed the time of day for a few minutes while Mary ran from room to room, looking for the rest of the family.

A couple of minutes later, Annie bent down and pulled a folded sheet of paper from her bag by the chair. She reached out across the table and put it into my hand.

"I'll be away the noo," shouted a voice from the hall.

"See you at the back o' five," replied Annie, without looking away from the paper in my hand.

"I thought you'd like to know what happened to me last Sunday," she said. "It's too long to share so I've written it down."

I thanked her and opened up the folded A4 sheet of paper. What follows is what I read…

Last Sunday was an awesome time. What God has done in my life has been amazing. I can now say that I have complete forgiveness for people I have struggled to forgive for many years. God has been doing a work in me for a long time and I know that on Sunday, I was finally able to let go of all those years of pain. This is my story:

"I was seven years old when I moved to Shettleston. There was a man living nearby, and I used to run errands for him and he used to give me money for sweets. One day he asked me to go to his house. He was very kind to me at first and then things began to change. He started to ask me to remove items of my clothing and walk round as though I were in some kind

of show. As more clothes came off, he took photos and then other things happened.

When I was eight, we moved house so I didn't need to see the guy anymore, but I remember the man downstairs giving me sweets. One day he bought two white mice and said I could visit them whenever I wanted. I started to go to see the mice. One thing led to another and I was caught in the same trap. One day Jimmy met me at lunch time and took me out of school. When I got back, the police were waiting and they took me to stand in a close and wait for him to come. When he came, they took him away and asked me lots of questions. When I got home, I was belted by my mother, she said I should never get involved with the police again!

At that time, there was a man who lived in the same house as us, who kept asking me to his room. By this time it was normal for me to follow these requests and also to comply with his requirements when I got to the room. I was so scared of him. I could smell cigarettes and alcohol on his breath whenever he was close. I was still eight years old.

One day my mum brought a man home. He ended up staying with us for four years and we called him our step dad. He used to visit me in the night but I was terrified to tell anyone. I think my brothers knew because they slept in the same room. I was terrified to go to sleep at night and I lay awake waiting for him to come in. I was tired and I started to skip school and when my step dad found out, he hit me with a belt.

I was glad to be in the same room at night as my brothers even though they bullied me. We had no toilet so we shared a bucket. One night they went on and on saying if I didn't drink the urine, they would tell tales to mum, so I drunk it.

I was so ashamed of my way of life. I was still only nine years old.

The Seagull

A few months later I was introduced to the man downstairs. He was very kind and my sister and I would go and visit him in his room. It was a small room down in the basement, his window was beneath the outside stairs. Things had been happening for a while and one day I said I wanted money, and amazingly he complied. It got to the point where he paid me to continue. This happened more than once. I told my sister what she could do to get money and she came down with me as she had done at first.

The house we lived in at that time was owned by a couple who had a grown up son who had his own room in the house. I was 11 and I used to go to visit him. He would show me things in his room. Then one day, he lit a candle and locked the door. Then he raped me. I was terrified and crying and telling myself I asked for it. He never touched me after that and I never told a soul.

I was 12 years old when we moved to Easterhouse. It was really good to have our own house. I used to help with the housework, trying to untangle the heavy woollen blankets and make the bed and I cleaned the brasses too. We used to fight to fill the coal scuttle as you got to batter the lumps of coal in the coal cupboard on the landing.

Easterhouse was great. We had three bedrooms, bathroom and kitchen. It all seemed so big. Everyone seemed to come from somewhere different and there were lots of new people to meet. The vans used to come round selling milk, ice cream and fruit and vegetables. They all went round the scheme. Of course there was the 'slate' to encourage us to buy whether we could afford it or not.

I shared a room with my sister and things started to look different. Then we met Stan. He stayed in the next close. He was married and had a two year old daughter and a baby on the way. I used to enjoy visiting them and baby sitting. Then after a while things began to change. He started acting differently and even more friendly. Then he and his family moved a little way away. One night he was taking me home in the car. I was in the back of the car and after a few minutes he stopped the car, got out and came into the back seat. The rest is history. They moved again shortly after that..."

The writing went on to describe a catalogue of invents that had continued, way into her twenties. It concluded:

"God has spent hours ministering His healing into the deepest parts of my life and as I said at the start, I feel now that I can totally let go of the past and look towards my future in Him."

I looked across at the woman sitting opposite me. One child, who would have chosen a life so very different, but who, by the grace of God, had fought through. I had not known Annie during those tragic years of childhood and adolescence but I had seen what God had done since.

Actually I marvelled at what I had seen God do not only in this life, but in many lives over and over again. And it wasn't the counselling, it wasn't the meetings, it wasn't the prayer although all these played a big part. The answer for Annie seemed to be, when "soaking" became part of her experience.

What is "soaking"? It is finding a place where we can become quiet before God to soak in His Holy Spirit and allow Him to do what He does best. Again and again, with quiet worship music, she was drawn nearer to God, as she soaked. Again and again she allowed the Great Physician to come close, allowing Him to carry out a divine heart transplant and bring healing to the deepest places within that heart.

Soaking, for Annie, eased her pain, gave her direction, lifted the burden of guilt and shame, empowered her to break free, gave her grace and patience for her life, helped her begin to move in the gifts of the Spirit and gave her more and more

91

intimacy with her Heavenly Father. Soaking in the Father's love changed her life.

Now, married for many years with a family of her own who are forming families of their own, it is a real testimony to letting God loose, to do what He does best.

...

Do you always mean to take time out, to relax, to slow down? Is it something that's always intended but something that's never done?

Why don't you begin to soak in God's presence, be saturated, marinated in the Holy Spirit and allow Him to penetrate every part of your life. It could change your life and if you do, it just might.

Sit or lie, use worship music or silence, but begin to regularly allow your Father in Heaven to put your life into perspective, in fact, to show you His perspective. We can become so easily separated from what is going on inside. Allow Him access to your inner world. He will bless you physically, mentally, emotionally and spiritually when you do.

Can you afford to miss it? Why don't you begin right now? Start by praying the prayer below then take as long as you have, to soak in His presence.

...

Prayer:

Father, you know my life and you know the many responsibilities I undertake. Important or urgent, I am always trying to decide.

Lord, there are so many things to do, and so little time. But Father I want to begin today to seek your presence in a greater way. Right now, in the quietness of this place, I welcome you Holy Spirit. You are welcome in my life right now. Come and indwell my spirit, my mind, my emotions and my physical frame too. Lord, I ask you to soak me, saturate me, marinate me in your Holy Spirit. Come, Holy Spirit, come...

Now take time with God and soak in His Holy Spirit.

The Truth about Soaking	
Psalm 23:2-3	You have bedded me down in lush meadows, you find me quiet pools to drink from. True to your word, you let me catch my breath and send me in the right direction.
Psalm 37:7	Quiet down before God, be prayerful before Him.
Psalm 46:10	Step out of the traffic! Take a long, loving look at me, your high God, above politics, above everything.
Isaiah 40:31	But those who wait upon God get fresh strength. They spread their wings and soar like eagles. They run and don't get tired, they walk and don't lag behind.
Isaiah 55:1	Hey there! All who are thirsty, come to the water! Are you penniless? Come anyway – buy and eat! Come buy your drinks, buy wine and milk. Buy without money – everything's free!
Matthew 1:28	Are you tired? Worn out? Burned out on religion? Come to me. Get away with me and you'll recover your life. I'll show you how to take a real rest.

Personal Notes:

The Seagull

Chapter 9

The Man in the Window
The Neighbour's Story

Sowing and reaping

The man looked at me with a curious look on his face. He wore a white apron and held a knife in his hand

"What do you mean?" he asked for a second time.

"Please could I have half a pound of stew and kidney?" I repeated.

"Not a clue what you want," he stated patiently. I tried again.

"Meat in gravy with vegetable in."

"Steak," he said. "You want steak."

"Fine," I said as the queue grew behind me.

"Anything else, hen?" he asked.

"Bacon," I replied. "Half a pound of bacon please."

"Right, hen," said the butcher reaching for the ham.

"No, bacon," I said.

"This *is* bacon," said the patient butcher.

"Fine, whatever it is, I want it," I replied, as I eyed the growing queue behind me. I was yet to learn that my bacon was their ham and my gammon was their bacon. I was also to learn that tatties were potatoes, neeps were turnips, pieces were sandwiches and a fizzy drink was ginger, a take away was a carry out and if I asked for sausage, it would probably be square!

We lived just across the road from the butcher. Every day I would cross the road and visit the shop. Sometimes the shop was full and the air too, was full with Glaswegian patter and local gossip. Sometimes it was empty and I would ask for my requests and leave. But how I longed to be part of the people.

Sometimes crossing the road was quite a long ordeal and it would be a while before a space would come in the traffic and I could cross to the four in a block downstairs flat where we lived.

We had asked the church to secure us somewhere to stay in the short term for our first year or so in Glasgow, and they had chosen a nice newly decorated glowing, white, downstairs apartment. It was very nice, apart from the parties!

Upstairs lived some avid Abba fans and once a month on the dot, parties going on till four or five in the morning, would take place in the apartment above us. Pulsating music would come through the ceiling, always on a Saturday night and many a month our preparation for a Sunday service became a cup of tea about three in the morning and a chat till five! Often we arrived at church baggy eyed humming *Voulez vous* and *Does your mother know?* as we prepared for the service.

About four months after we moved into Croftfoot, there was a shot gun robbery in the post office across the road. As mentioned before, violence is a part of Glasgow life. From the "bread and beer riots" in the eighteenth and nineteenth centuries, gang warfare in the nineteen-twenties and thirties, to knife carrying and the trend of violence for thrills in the twenty-first century, violence unfortunately has a part in Glasgow culture. At the time of the shot gun robbery, we had a visitor staying with us. We never saw her again!

I used to visit the post office every day to post letters back home to the Midlands where we had lived for over thirty years.

It was one February morning when I had made my daily visit to R S McColl's and I was crossing the road back to the house. I looked up the road towards Castlemilk.

Castlemilk (known locally as "the milk"), was one of the largest housing schemes in Europe when it was built in the 1950s. Castlemilk too, is an area which has had much gang activity through the years since it was built. The root cause of much of the gang warfare has been territory disputes. Gangs have their own area of the city which they defend sometimes to the death. Through the years, Castlemilk became the home of Castlemilk Cumbie, Castlemilk Fleet, Castlemilk To and Castlemilk Young Team. Church members who lived in the area recounted dog fights, washing stolen off the washing line and toys taken from their children playing in the close.

"It's a great way to get to know your neighbours," we were told. "Watching the regular fights in the street, we must wave at each other at least twice a week!"

Walking past the bus stop, I neared our own house. I could see Michael, our ten year old dog, standing on the settee, nose pressed to the window patiently awaiting my arrival. I neared our house and as I did, I glanced to my left to the house next door to ours. As I did, I caught sight of a man sitting behind the window pane looking out into the street. I smiled and lifted my hand, and he smiled back and waved too. Our eyes met briefly for a few moments and then I continued on, lost in my own thoughts of home many miles away. I reached our garden gate and walked up the path.

I thought no more about the man in the window. I never saw him again. Day after day as I passed that way, occasionally I glanced to the house but he was never there. Winter turned to spring and then to summer and the weather improved a little. Summer seemed very similar to all the other seasons in Glasgow, except that it didn't snow. Apart from that, there often wasn't much difference.

Thursday morning dawned fair and bright and I was removing the washing from the washing machine. I glanced out of the window and saw the sun creeping from behind the clouds, so I decided to hang the washing outside in the shared garden at the back of the flats.

Each back garden was divided into two, with a fence from the house to the bottom of the garden. I lifted the wet bundle from the machine and into our blue plastic basket and carried it out of the side door and round the back into the garden. I began to hang the washing on the clothes line and as I did, I noticed a lady in the garden next door.

"How are you?" I asked, as she glanced in my direction.

"Ah, not so good, my man passed away last week so I'm not so good just now."

"I'm sorry to hear that," I replied, feeling sudden compassion for the stranger across the fence.

"Sorry it's not been a good time for you," I said, looking to continue the conversation.

"Aye," she replied, "Must admit I've had more than a wee bubble this month."

"Actually, I wanted to thank you," she continued.

"Thank me?" I questioned. I was interested, as I could think of no contact I had had with this lady before today.

"Aye," she continued, "There was one morning you were walking along and you waved at my man and smiled. He was so thrilled, saw no one at all and he talked about that continually after that. He was bedridden soon after but still talked of it. I'll need to go," she continued. "Minister's comin' the back o' three and ma heids full o' mince…"

I stood and watched her go inside, at that moment wishing with all my heart I had made an effort to do more, to know these folk who lived next door... visit... help... anything. Instead, the last few months I had lived in a world of my own, surrounded by feelings of loss and feeling as if I was at the end of my world, instead of looking up and realizing I was just at the beginning.

I knew that if I had taken time to sow something good into the lives of others at that time, I would have reaped a sense of belonging, of identity and of satisfaction that it took me months to achieve.

The man in the window taught me a lot although he never knew it. Right next door to me as I cried for my family, there was a man and woman who cried for their life and I never took the trouble to see them.

We moved round the corner shortly after that, but I never forgot the man at the window and his wife.

...

Are you looking for opportunities to sow? There is an undisputable principle in the Bible called "sowing and reaping". If you sow, you will reap. It may not come back in the same form but whether it's money, time, love, ability or whatever, you will end up the better for it. Why don't you increase the sowing in your life, not for what you'll get, but just because Jesus loves you to do it?

...

Look at the boxes below. Record in the yesterday box the names of six or more people and any way you sowed into their lives yesterday or before.

Now look at the tomorrow box and list those you know you will meet. Ask God to show you ways you can be a blessing to them in what you do or what you say and record it next to their names.

Return to this in the future and add others you meet and ways God allows you to bless them.

Yesterday	Tomorrow

Begin everyday to sow into the lives of others in a greater way from today onwards.

Prayer:

Father, I pray that you will give me divine opportunities tomorrow, to sow into the lives of others in a greater way than yesterday. Lord, let all I do and say, enrich those I meet. In Jesus' name, Amen.

The Truth about Sowing and Reaping	
Hosea 10:12	Sow righteousness, reap love.
Luke 6:31	Live generously.
Luke 6:35	I tell you, love your enemies. Help and give without expecting a return. You'll never regret it – I promise.
Luke 6:37-38	Give away your life; you'll find life given back, but not merely given back – given back with bonus and blessing. Giving, not getting, is the way. Generosity begets generosity.
2 Corinthians 9:6,7a,8	A stingy planter gets a stingy crop; a lavish planter gets a lavish crop. God loves it when the giver delights in the giving. God can pour on the blessings in astonishing ways so that you're ready for anything and everything, more than just ready to do what needs to be done.
Galatians 6:7b-8	What a person plants, he will harvest. The person who plants selfishness, ignoring the needs of others-ignoring God-harvests a crop of weeds. All He'll have to show for his life is weeds! But the one who plants in response to God, letting God's Spirit do the growth work in him, harvests a crop of real, eternal life.

Personal Notes:

Chapter 10

The Platonic Baby
Ally's Story

Performance orientation

I peered around the door frame into the room before me. Inside was a middle aged lady with a sweeping brush, busily sweeping the polished floor beneath her feet. She looked across and then smiled and continued her task. I turned and wandered down the passage way. All around, in every room, people were hoovering, dusting, tidying and polishing ready for the arrival of the new pastor. It was July 1990.

Kevin, who was going to be the new pastor, had in fact arrived in Glasgow a few days before but tomorrow night was to be the induction service. He and I were just passing and popped in to say "hello".

The Glasgow church building was built in 1984, after many moves in its long history. Always on the south side of the city and always in some old building the church moved from place to place seeking a home of its own. Numbers varied. In 1941 the church went from 500 to 50 people in one week as most of the people left to follow George Jeffreys, Elim's founder. He left Elim to form the Bible Pattern denomination. The days were not easy and many sacrifices were made to ensure the survival of the church in Govanhill. As the 1960's, 70's and 80's passed the numbers steadily rose, and in the 1980s the church was averaging 60-70 and secured its own newly built building. God was about to do new things. But that was in the past and now it was the start of the 90's.

I stood in the doorway of the sanctuary, a square room with a stage at the opposite end from where I stood. On the left was a piano and on the right was an organ but various guitars left around and a drum set at the side showed signs that the church had transitioned into the new worship of the early 90s.

"Hello," a voice said, pulling me out of my observations.

"Hello," I replied turning to look at a tall thin girl in front of me.

Ally had brown hair and freckles and a cheeky grin on her face.

"Are you new?" she asked with a questioning look on her face.

"I am," I replied. "I'm married to the new pastor. Pleased to meet you," and I smiled at the small, brown eyes before me. Then I turned to walk away.

"Does he dance?" she suddenly blurted out.

"Sorry?" I questioned and turned again to where she was standing.

"Does he dance?" she said. "If he doesna dance in the worship then I'll be away – and a whole load more of us too," and with that she turned and walked back down the corridor. That was my first meeting with Ally.

I got to knew Ally a little better as time went by. One day, she told me about her past. She told me about her experience of life as a mother, of how that first time she held her child in her arms and she felt she would burst with joy, of the days and months of having, for the first time, someone to love and care for, something that was totally dependent on her, something she would die for.

Little Sammy was her reason for living. Even on the darkest day, one smile from him made the struggle all worthwhile. And a struggle it was. Money was scarce and bills were high and many a night Ally went to sleep hungry to ensure that Sammy ate well. And yet as time went by it seemed that the "brew" never went far enough and one wet Monday afternoon, they arrived home to find the locks changed and their few possessions piled up outside on the street. Joining the endless queues outside the hostel for women and children was the only thing to do – her friends had problems of their own.

"I want to go home," cried Sammy one night after she had tucked him into his little hostel bed.

"I want to go home," he sobbed as large tears rolled down his little face.

Even larger ones rolled down the face of Ally that night as she watched her child as he slept peacefully clutching his old toy rabbit. How she wished for him a nice home, piles of toys in the corner and a daddy who came home every night.

It seemed that things only got worse and it was mid February when Ally found herself awaiting an hour that would change her life forever.

She had managed to secure a bed-sit for Sammy and herself and get a few hours work down at the local store to pay the rent. Her only problem was child care for Sammy. Just a couple of hours alone each day wouldn't hurt him surely? He was a good child and waited patiently for his mother to come home each evening. But the neighbour across the landing knew that that was no good for a five year old boy and the rest is history...

And so Ally waited – the next few hours passed as a dream, a knock on the door, a smartly dressed lady, tears from the child and then Ally was left alone with only the memory of the beautiful big eyes pleading, "Mum don't let them take me, mum don't let them...don't let them do it!" Ally looked round the tiny bed-sit. His few clothes were gone and his few possessions lay scattered around. "At least he's got his rabbit," she thought, "at least he's got that," as she lay on the bed and sobbed her way through the night.

That was years before and now, several years later, Ally was in our church and part of our family. Yet that experience had a profound effect upon her life. Desperate to be accepted as part of this, her first real family, she was an approval addict. On top of the world when receiving acceptance but without constant approval from people, disillusionment would cause her to plummet. When she felt unable to earn love, it led to the black hole of anger and disappointment. Then the thought, "maybe if I do something to get back on track," provided a fix of love which motivated her to more work and get more rewards. Back on top of the world with approval and acceptance, the circle began again. Only as her knowledge of God's love increased was she able to begin to let go of striving and performance, and rest in the knowledge that it doesn't matter what others think.

Although doing her best to perform, she still often needed a little guidance in life. On one occasion a lady rushed into the office quite perturbed.

"Whatever's wrong?" I asked, looking at her flustered features.

"I've just been asked out," said the distressed woman.

"That's not such a bad thing is it?" I answered, knowing she was single and would really like to meet someone.

"What happened?" I continued.

"I was outside the kitchen door and a tall, young woman came up to me and said, 'There's someone in the church that likes you.' I said, 'Who?' She said, 'Me, can I take you to the cinema on Friday?'"

"Ally," said Kevin, a few minutes later after we located her in the kitchen.

"I don't want you propositioning women in the church."

"Don't worry, Pastor," she replied, "I've got great respect Pastor. I'd never touch another woman up…at least not in the church." And with that, she flounced out of the office.

We didn't know about Ally's sexual orientation until that point and we didn't know about her mother's either until she came to live with Ally in the hostel opposite the church. Jackie, also a practising lesbian, came to thank us on the first day she moved to Glasgow. Thick set, speaking with an Irish accent, she made her way to Kevin's office one Wednesday lunch time.

"I just wanted to thank you for all you've done for Ally," she said. "Changed girl," she added, "Changed girl."

"No problem," said Kevin. "No problem at all. We're glad to have her."

We could never actually pin Ally down as to whether she'd ever made a decision to go for God but she was certainly part of the church and all that went on there.

…

Someone else who was part of the church was Des Owen. Des had come over from Ireland a couple of years before. Unlike Ally, he was not forthcoming about his past life and seemed reluctant to let us know anything about it. We only knew he had needed to leave Ireland suddenly and wouldn't be returning.

Des and Ally were firm friends. As Des was homosexual and Ally chose women over men, it was a purely platonic relationship. They were rarely apart both at church and it seemed outside, and they seemed to find consolation in each others' company. Purely platonic they maintained.

And then one morning they called in to give us some news.

"I thought you'd be pleased," said Des with a huge grin covering his face. For a moment, Kevin was speechless.

"Yes, it's true," joined in Ally "I'm preggers. We've got the photo. It's a toty wee thing just now but it'll grow," she said with pride.

We didn't actually know whether to congratulate them on moving one step nearer to a biblical lifestyle or chastise them for having slipped from the biblical lifestyle.

Des and Ally went on to marry and have a beautiful baby son. I looked down at him shortly after he was born. I wished for him a lovely home and piles of toys in the corner and a daddy who would come home every night. I know that Ally wished the same.

They moved from Glasgow a while later. I don't know what happened after that but I hope they made it. I doubt it – but I hope they did!

...

Maybe your life is nothing like Ally's. But how is your need to perform? Do you recognise the pattern? Do you have a tendency to fall back into striving by your human effort? You have the gift of salvation, but has your heart kept its habit to earn love by performing? Do you live your life with motives other than God's love driving you to serve Him through striving and tension and fear?

Whose approval do you seek, your pastor's, your friends', your spouse's? Allow God to change that today and let Him become the only motive for all you do and for all you are. May His unconditional love come, and dwell in you like never before.

...

Prayer:
Father, as I take this time with you, would you do what I cannot do? Let me see today that your love is not conditional on my striving to be the first or the best or the strongest or the fastest. Thank you that when I take refuge in you, I will lack nothing. In Jesus' name, Amen.

Now take time to meditate on the verses of scripture below. Meditate on the key words...taste, see, blessed, refuge, fear nothing, seek, no good thing etc...

Allow God access to minister into the deep places of your heart with His unconditional love.

Passage for meditation: "Taste and see that the Lord is good; blessed are those who take refuge in Him. Fear the Lord; you His holy people for those who fear Him lack nothing. The lions may grow weak and hungry, but those who seek the Lord lack no good thing," Psalm 34:8-18.

The Truth about Performance Orientation	
Matthew 1:29b	Learn the unforced rhythms of grace. I won't lay anything heavy or ill-fitting on you. Keep company with me and you'll learn to live freely and lightly.
Matthew 11:28-29	Are you tired? Worn out? Burned out on religion? Come to me. Come away with me and you'll recover your life. I'll show you how to take a real rest. Walk with me and work with me – watch how I do it.
Galatians 1:10	Do you think I speak this strongly in order to manipulate crowds? Or carry favour with God? Or get popular applause? If my goal was popularity. I wouldn't bother being Christ's slave.
Galatians 3:5	Answer this question: Does the God who lavishly provides you with His own presence, His Holy Spirit, working things in your lives you could never do for yourselves, does He do these things because of your strenuous moral striving or because you trust Him to do them in you?
Galatians 3:22	...to show us the futility of devising some religious system for getting by our own efforts what we can only get by waiting in faith for God to complete His promise.
2 Corinthians 12:9	My grace is enough; it's all you need. My strength comes into its own in your weakness.

Personal Notes:

The Seagull

Chapter 11

The Tea Towel
The Pastor's Story

Breaking out of your comfort zone

"Fifteen, sixteen, seventeen, eighteen..." I continued to count.

"Nineteen, twenty, twenty-one, twenty-two..." I eyed the suitcases being placed on the floor beside me.

The airport baggage room was crowded and for a few moments, I lost sight of the people I had just met off the plane.

A few minutes earlier, we had searched through the many tired faces who were then entering the arrivals hall until we recognised faces we knew and walked forward to become part of the kissing and hugging crowd before us.

Sam Kelp had visited our church along with his wife and children several times. This time, in addition to those, he brought thirty-seven suitcases too, filled not only with clothes, but with books, tapes and CDs, which would be sold during the conference meetings.

At long last, we had every suitcase accounted for, and packed ourselves, plus luggage, into the two cars and minibus we had brought with us. The weekend was about to begin.

Sitting in the passenger side of the minibus, I watched as we joined the M8 and the lines of traffic heading towards Glasgow.

I glanced at my watch and then looked up, grateful that it was only 2.20pm. I knew that by half past two, the lanes of traffic would have slowed almost to a stop, as hundreds of cars headed towards the Kingston Bridge on their way to Edinburgh or somewhere in that direction. The traffic was still flowing well as we moved into the outside lane. We changed lanes again to leave the motorway at Junction 21 and the cars sped past us.

My mind went back to the last visit of Sam Kelp to our church. We had spent a few days touring Scotland with Sam and four little Kelps. I remembered how at each photo opportunity, the van would screech to a halt and out would pile the Kelps, Sam with camera in hand and little Kelps anywhere and everywhere. I smiled as I remembered being a nervous wreck by the end of the trip after many times, trying to explain that although Scottish country roads look deserted, that in a moment a speeding car can come from any direction. I was always relieved when we had collected all the little Kelps once again into the minibus and had them safely back in suburbia.

My mind returned to the present time as we drove up Eglinton Road and onto Cumberland Street, past the tall towering blocks of flats which had replaced the dark rows of tenements in the Gorbals area. Now, there was even the New Gorbals with its designer homes and the hanging angel which, a couple of years ago, had drawn news crews from miles around as they investigated whether or not, it was dripping blood. It turned out to be rust!

We began the weekend on the Friday evening. Our church had never failed to be mightily impacted by the ministry of Sam and Davina and all the extra arrangements were a price well worth paying.

It was a hot and sultry Sunday night and people had already begun arriving for the final meeting of the weekend. Groups of people stood about, talking, while a couple of the praise band was tuning up on the platform and a few others were buying some of the books which had come out of the thirty seven suitcases.

Before long, the meeting was underway. The church was packed with conference goers and also our usual Sunday evening congregation. The praise progressed to worship which in turn brought about a rich presence of God.

It was unusual for me to be on the front row. I much preferred sitting at the back, looking round for who was at the services. Newcomers were a high priority to us and there were always new faces to be sought out after the service. At the front, I was unable to look round in the usual way but I enjoyed the increase in atmosphere and it was great to watch this anointed couple in action, in close up. Exactly one hour later, the church was quiet as the congregation sat listening intently to Sam as he preached about Joshua marching round the walls of Jericho. I watched as sweat trickled down Sam's face, as he brought the Word of God powerfully to the people. We were nearing the end of the service.

"And I am asking you, are you willing to make a shout when God says 'Shout'?" he asked the congregation.

I glanced at the clock and tried to remember if I had taken the sausage rolls from the freezer.

"What is your shout?" continued Sam in full flow.

"What is it that would stretch you, really stretch you? Well – that's going to be your shout!"

"Amen," the people responded from various parts of the room, gripped by the charismatic style of preaching as well as by the Spirit of God in those moments.

"Twenty past eight," I looked again at the clock to my right.

"He's closing early tonight," I thought, thinking that he may be tired from the weekend's frantic pace. I looked around at the people and knew they would happily sit there for much longer.

"We'll have a march!" Sam's words suddenly caught my attention.

"Yes, we'll have a march – as Joshua did around Jericho."

We spent the next few minutes putting chairs to the side, moving handbags and coats and generally clearing the centre of the church until nothing remained except the carpeted floor.

I watched as people, unsure of what to do next, hovered around the chairs and some headed for the toilet.

A group of our intercessors stood excitedly near the platform. I knew, having waited years for this moment, they were not going to miss it.

Others stood, back to the wall, quite obviously already well out of their comfort zone and Kevin, having headed for the platform, was busily leafing through his Bible.

Quite happy though, for his church to march, he took up position to survey the scene.

"Right," said Sam, when the room was satisfactorily organised. "If we're having a march, then a march needs a leader." And he looked round the room.

His eyes came to rest on the platform. He turned, pointed to Kevin and said, "You...you are the leader."

Kevin looked up from the book of Joshua, as he thought quickly for an excuse to escape, mentally halving Sam's ministry gift as he did! It seemed that no excuse came because a minute later, he could be found at the head of a procession of rabid intercessors and prophets.

Once in place, Sam turned again to Kevin.

"If you're the leader, then you need a banner. Where are the banners!?" he exclaimed.

"We don't have any banners," replied Kevin, obviously already well out of his comfort zone by the tone in his voice.

Sam responded by looking round, bending and picking something from the left hand side of the stage. He thrust it into Kevin's hand. It was a tea towel.

"There's your banner," he said. "Now, lead the march!"

Kevin at that moment looked as though he would love the experience of Enoch, to be transported somewhere else, but as that prayer wasn't answered, there was nothing for it but to march.

The leader began, looking to all the world like a six foot, one inch man, waving a tea towel followed by a string of women who were already interceding and praising God. As they rounded the first bend, the intercessors were already going for it, breaking strongholds and shouting their prayers to the heavenlies.

Several men were pinned to the far wall. Jim, one of our leaders, arms folded, slight amusement in his eyes, regarded

Kevin cautiously. He had a bubble coming out of his head which said, "Yes, Pastor, you do look a plonker!"

The group rounded the bend again and headed up the stage side of the church. I caught Kevin's eye as he passed the lectern. He flicked his head sideways as though to say, "Get over here."

I chose to look the other way, and busy myself watching the great crowd of witnesses which followed behind! The line reached the next bend and rounded back at the bottom end of the church. I saw Kevin glance over at the door, wondering just how many people he was losing at this moment. He passed a deacon, who remarkably also seemed pinned to the wall.

"You're on your own pal," said the bubble coming out of his head.

And so the march continued round and round. The atmosphere was charged with noisy intercession and loud praise music accompanied the proceedings.

Suddenly, I looked again at the leader with the tea towel. There had been a change. I began to notice that no longer was he feebly waving it occasionally from side to side. But something different was happening.

In his own words:

"I suddenly thought, 'Here I am, circling the room with my eyes fixed on everyone at the side and my mind fixed on what will people think?' Why don't I do what the man said – and pray for the breaking of barriers and walls within and around this church. So that's what I did. I began to pray. 'Lord, I come against those powers and principalities that would seek to...' and you know, in my spirit, the tea towel became a sword, and I saw the words of the intercessors behind me having a powerful effect on the things they were coming

against. Those at the sides faded away as we went a fourth, fifth, sixth and seventh time round the church."

After seven times round, Sam shouted for everyone to stop.

"No!" shouted Kevin, "Let's not stop yet...the first three times don't count!"

Nothing was ever quite the same after that night. It seems a very simple thing to do nowadays, but on that night we had broken through out of our comfort zone into a new level of powerful encounters of God.

It was just one of those times when our extraordinary God takes an ordinary moment and is able to do something amazing in the Spirit.

Comfort zones are pretty comfortable places. Many people left theirs that night and were changed on their journey towards glory.

...

Do you have a fear of man? Earnestly ask yourself, are you willing to leave your comfort zone in order to step out into new things, if God so desires?

The Bible says, *"The fear of man is a snare."* Are there snares around you, in front, behind and to the side – a boundary of your own fear to step across the line and be radical for God? Many Bible people had to break down the fear of man – Daniel, Elijah, Ezekiel, Peter, Paul and many more. Why don't you ask God to speak into this area in your life and set you free to leave your comfort zone today?

...

Prayer:

Father God,
I thank you for the safe place you have provided for me in you. But, Lord, right now, I confess that sometimes, I get comfortable and I am not prepared to leave that comfort. Lord, I pray that you will show me those times or those people who intimidate me and cause me to stay where I am. Help me to break free from the fear of man and hear when you call me.

Now ask Him to reveal to you anyone who intimidates what you do or say in the things of God

List them below:

Lord, I bring these people before you and I repent for their effect on my words and my actions. Please forgive me when I have not said what you asked me to say or done what you asked me to do.

I forgive them for the times I have allowed them to intimidate me physically or mentally and I release them into the freedom of my forgiveness.

I ask you now to take the Sword of the Spirit and to break down the snares of fear which surround me. Lord, I thank you for what you are doing right now.

I ask that as you make the way ahead smooth before me, that you fill me with your Holy Spirit as I seek to say what you ask me to say and do what you ask me to do.
In Jesus' name I pray, Amen.

The Truth About Stepping Out of Your Comfort Zone	
Deuteronomy 31:6	Be strong. Take courage. Don't be intimidated. Don't give them a second thought because God, your God, is striding ahead of you. He's right there with you. He won't let you down; He won't leave you.
1 Chronicles 22:13b	Courage! Take charge! Don't be timid; don't hold back.
Psalm 18:28-29	Suddenly, God, you floodlight my life. I'm blazing with glory, God's glory! I smash the bands of marauders, I vault the highest fences.
Psalm 118:6	God's now at my side and I'm not afraid; who would dare lay a hand on me?
Proverbs 29:25	The fear of human opinion disables; trusting in God protects you from that.
Philippians 4:13	Whatever I have, wherever I am, I can make it through anything in the One who makes me who I am.

....

The Seagull

Epilogue

It was exactly one year later that I went back to Shetland.

It wasn't long before I found myself walking along the beautiful white beach, watching the waves and feeling the wind on my face.

As I wandered along the seashore, I looked ahead, searching with my eyes for the nest of one year ago.

Eventually, I reached that cliff once again and stood below the nest. It looked old and windswept and it was empty. I waited and watched, just hoping against hope that maybe my seagull would be here.

But suddenly, I realised, that's not how it was meant to be. I turned from the nest and gazed into the sky above. The nest was empty but as I stood, I began to realise that someplace, somewhere, there was a seagull flying high.

I read the other day that seagulls live for ten, twenty or sometimes, even thirty years. That means she could be alive today. And if she is I know that wherever she may be now, she will have built her own nest, watched other eggs crack open, helped other little birds start to fly and in addition to all those things, she will be soaring high, doing what she loves and what she was created to do.

And in the same way, there are many people I have seen and will see, who have and will fly far higher than I, doing what they were created to do. They fly in attitude and choice. They fly with mercy and words of love. They fly by soaking and sowing and they fly way out of their comfort zone. They do what they are created to do.

Up through the atmosphere…up where the air is clear.

Do what you are created to do.

FLY HIGH!

FLY HIGH!

A New Chapter

If you've never actually begun a relationship with God and after reading this book, you are beginning to wonder if there is a Father God in heaven. If you're beginning to wonder if there is a God who you need to get to know, then use the prayer below to start a new chapter in your life.

Dear God
You know all about me.
You that I'm not even sure you exist. Yet you love me all the same.
Today, I want to join your family and become your child.
I confess my wrong doing and I bring it to your cross.
I ask you to forgive those things, and I ask you to clean up me life.
I acknowledge that you sent your Son to die on a cross, to same me from hell and to give me a life in heaven.
I want to fly high in my life.
I want to soar the heights and fulfil every potential you put in me.
I make a choice to turn from everything that will hold me down.
I ask today that you become my Lord and I ask you to begin a new chapter in my life.
In Jesus Name,
Amen.

It's time for you to begin to fly….

If you need details of a church near you
Please e-mail me on KMPeat@aol.com

The Seagull

Appendix 1

Personal Testimonies
Angels and things
(chapter 6)

"The communion table was at the front. I didn't know or understand what was happening; all I knew was that people were piling up on the floor under the presence of God.

During the fourteen days ablaze, some people were falling over under the power of God when they got out of the cars in the car park. Other people saw angels around the church. One guy, a non Christian, left with his girlfriend and when he got in the car, he started speaking in tongues. He'd never heard of such a thing and didn't know what was happening. His girlfriend brought him back into the church where he got saved. This didn't fit in with our theology at all!" – M

"People saw angels in the car park as they were arriving at church. I remember because it was on the same day I was stuck to the floor unable to move for a couple of hours because there was such a heavy presence in the place. There was such an amazing presence of God and it was then for the first time, that I felt that someone cared for me. Coming from violent parents, sexual abuse etc that meant a lot." – P

"The axe head was above Kevin on the ceiling and we all started to point to it. I often talk about that, still, because it was awesome. The hairs on the back of my neck stood up! I just sat and looked at it for what seemed like ages until it disappeared." – M

"My hands were burning and my back. I remember saying, if this isn't God, I must be ill! I also remember my husband half carrying me out to the car one night after the service. I couldn't stand and when we got to the car, he had left his keys in church. He draped me over the bonnet of the car and went back in for his keys." – O

"I remember spending half the service in the loo as I couldn't get off the floor in there. It was a real time of healing and freedom. God gave me an axe! A very strange idea – a wee Glasga' wumin with an axe!" – A

"I was standing at the keyboard leading the worship that night. Kevin lifted his hands up and never even said a word. It was more than a wind; there was a low frequency noise that I can only describe as a pulse which came from the curtains behind me. There was a gust of wind and suddenly, an entire row of people who had been standing, were lying on the floor bowled over." – E

"Kevin was in full flight preaching – my eye was drawn to the top of the curtains behind him – a mist was forming. It began to thicken and then to gently cascade downwards. It formed like a wave around Kevin, wherever he went it went, ahead of him, above him, behind him. The cloud then loomed above Kevin and began to develop a recognisable humanlike form; it was about 2.5 metres high.

The face took on clearer features. I ran out of the sanctuary in tears and in panic. I bumped into Margaret and tried to explain my experience. She invited me back into the sanctuary and I hesitantly agreed. Margaret asked me if it was still there. It was. When men see angels in the Bible, they say 'fear not'. I'm not surprised, I was very afraid!" – B

"I thought, at first, the wind was coming from the fire doors which were open next to me. Then there was this fragrance all around me. There was such a sense of wonder, awe, peace and healing. No one prayed for me or touched me except Jesus. I was crying with the beauty of the experience." – MA

"There were angelic visitations, physical manifestations, tears, laughter, strange phenomena, meetings that lasted into the wee small hours when we had work the next day and even deliverance in the midst of it all. I saw lives changed, people more in love with Jesus, people healed from pain and set free. At times it was weird and scary to be part of but would I do it again? Where do I sign up?!" – E

The Seagull

Appendix 2

A Mansion in Heaven (chapter 2)

Ungodly beliefs

1. I am not good enough to receive anything from God.

2. I am valuable because of what I do, not because I am me.

3. It is impossible for me to stop that habit.

4. I will always be sad/shy/insecure.

5. I have wasted years of my life and it is too late to change that.

6. No one cares what I feel or think.

7. I am alone and will always be on the outside.

8. I must keep my real feelings hidden. I cannot show who I really am.

9. There is no one to help me.

10. I can't risk getting close to anyone or I might get hurt.

11. God loves other people much more than me.

12. I can never be good enough to please God.

13. God is cross with me.

14. If I trust God, He will let me down.

15. Everyone uses me, no one appreciates me.

16. If I need help, there is no one to help me.

17. I will never be able to please God.

18. I will never change enough to be what God wants.

19. If people knew what I was really like, they would reject me.

20. I am inferior to other people around me.

The Patter

Away – go
Away wi the fairies – in a dream
Aye, that'll be right – there's no chance of that
Back o' – after
Bampot – an idiot or a fool
Bar L – nickname for Barlinne Prison
Bevvie – a beer
Brew – Social Security allowance
Bubble – to weep or cry
But – however
Cannae – can't
Carry out – take away food
Chap – knock (on the door)
Clap – stroke or pat
Da – Dad
Decanted – moved out from home for a period of time
Disnae – doesn't
Feart – frightened
Fish supper – two fish and a portion of chips
Footer – fiddle
Glasga' – Glasgow
Gauny – going to
Greet – to cry
Head's full o mince – can't think straight
Hen – a term of affection for a woman
How no'? – why not?
How's it gaun? – how is it going?

I'm just after – just finished
Janny – caretaker
Knock ye pan in – try too hard
Lose your rag – lose your temper
Ma – Mum
Ma man – My husband
Naw – no
Nippin ma heed – moaning
Pan loaf – an oblong loaf with a soft crust
Toty – little
Up to high doh – very worried
Wabbt – no energy
Winch – kiss and cuddle
Wumin – woman

I ask Him that with both feet planted firmly on love,
you'll be able to take in with all Christians the
extravagant dimensions of Christ's love.

Reach out and experience the breadth!
Test its length!
Plumb the depths!
Rise to the heights!
Live full lives, full in the fullness of God.

God can do anything, you know –
far more than you could ever imagine or guess
or request in your wildest dreams!
He does it not by pushing us around but by working
within us, His Spirit deeply and gently within us.

Glory to God in the church!
Glory to God in the Messiah, in Jesus!
Glory down all the generations!
Glory through all millennia!
Oh, yes!

Ephesians 3:17b-21

About the author:

Margaret Peat ministers alongside her husband, Kevin, in the Elim Churches in Scotland, North West England and North Wales. They moved to Glasgow in 1990 to minister in the Elim Church until 2004 when they began to oversee churches in the aforementioned areas. Together, they also regularly minister in New Zealand and Canada. Margaret has written one book before in 2005, called *The White Elephant*. She is also on the national team for Aspire, Elim's exciting initiative for women throughout the UK and beyond. Kevin and Margaret have been married for 29 years and live south of Glasgow in East Kilbride, Scotland.

The Seagull

The Seagull